WAR IN THE WORLD-SYSTEM

Recent Titles in
Contributions in Economics and Economic History

WAR IN THE WORLD-SYSTEM

EDITED BY
Robert K. Schaeffer

STUDIES IN THE POLITICAL ECONOMY
OF THE WORLD-SYSTEM
Immanuel Wallerstein, ADVISORY EDITOR

CONTRIBUTIONS IN ECONOMICS AND
ECONOMIC HISTORY, NUMBER 93

GREENWOOD PRESS
New York • Westport, Connecticut • London

Library of Congress Cataloging-in-Publication Data

War in the world-system.

(Studies in the political economy of the world-system) (Contributions in economics and economic history, ISSN 0084–9235 ; no. 93)
Bibliography: p.
Includes index.
1. Military history, Modern—Congresses. 2. War—Congresses. 3. History, Modern—Congresses.
4. Capitalism—Congresses. 5. Economic history—Congresses. I. Schaeffer, Robert K. II. Series.
III. Series: Contributions in economics and economic history ; no. 93.
U39.W37 1989   355′.02   88–35757
ISBN 0–313–25429–X (lib. bdg. : alk. paper)

British Library Cataloguing in Publication Data is available.

Library of Congress Catalog Card Number: 88–35757
ISBN: 0–313–25429–X
ISSN: 0084–9235

First published in 1989

Greenwood Press, Inc.
88 Post Road West, Westport, Connecticut 06881

Printed in the United States of America

∞™

The paper used in this book complies with the Permanent Paper Standard issued by the National Information Standards Organization (Z39.48–1984).

10 9 8 7 6 5 4 3 2 1

To Torry and Jazz Dickinson

Contents

SERIES FOREWORD

Immanuel Wallerstein

The Political Economy of the World-System section of the American Sociological Association was created in the 1970s to bring together a small but growing number of social scientists concerned with analyzing the processes of world-systems in general, and our modern one in particular.

Although organizationally located within the American Sociological Association, the PEWS Section bases its work on the relative insignificance of the traditional disciplinary boundaries. For that reason it has held an annual spring conference, open to and drawing participation from persons who work under multiple disciplinary labels.

For PEWS members, not only is our work unidisciplinary but the study of the world-system is not simply another "specialty" to be placed beside so many others. It is instead a different "perspective" with which to analyze all the traditional issues of the social sciences. Hence, the themes of successive PEWS conferences are quite varied and cover a wide gamut of topics. What they share is the sense that the isolation of political, economic, and socio-cultural "variables" is a dubious enterprise, that all analysis must be simultaneously historical and systemic, and that the conceptual bases of work in the historical social sciences must be rethought.

PREFACE

The chapters in this book were first presented at the twelfth annual Political Economy of the World-System Conference, which was held at Emory University in March 1988. Terry Boswell organized this conference around the theme "War and Revolution in the World-System." The research presented in Atlanta was then divided into two companion volumes: *Revolution in the World-System* and *War in the World-System*.

The scholars who participated in the conference and whose research is published here represent different disciplines, but they share a common concern about war and an interest in approaching the problems associated with war from a world-system perspective. There is no world-system canon to which they all subscribe, but they all view war within a global, historical context and seek to understand the social, political, and economic dynamics that contribute to war and peace in the modern world.

Terry Boswell deserves credit for organizing the conference, scrutinizing proposals, and collecting papers, some of which appear in this volume. I want to thank him for his formative contribution to this project and for asking me to edit this book.

The contributors to this volume also deserve thanks; they all engaged in serious discussion about their research and worked to advance the understanding of war in theoretical and empirical terms.

Immanuel Wallerstein, the series editor, provided useful criticism and editorial suggestions. Cynthia Harris and Lynn Flint at Greenwood Press skillfully ushered the book through the publication process. Torry Dickinson provided trenchant criticism of my work and useful commentary on other contributions. By shouldering other tasks, she made it possible for me to find time to complete this project.

WAR IN THE WORLD-SYSTEM

1

INTRODUCTION

Robert Schaeffer

A world-system approach to the study of war is historically bound. It is confined to the period since the emergence of capitalism in Europe and the development of what Immanuel Wallerstein calls the "modern world-system," which has its origins in the late fifteenth, sixteenth, and early seventeenth centuries. This approach, which confines the study of war to the last three or four hundred years, is more modest than some. It does not attempt to discover a single entelechy of war that can be reduced to transhistorical dictums such as Karl von Clausewitz's assertion that "war is the continuation of politics by other means" or Mao Tse-tung's claim that "the aim of war is to eliminate war" (1967, 80). Quite the contrary. The entelechics of Clausewitz and Mao must be understood as the product of war making in a particular historical period. They do not describe the war aims of the Ostrogoths or Genghis Khan, or, for that matter, those of the Mayans or Richard III.

If there is a transhistorical truth about war, it is that war kills, but this is true by definition. Wars kill in different ways and for very different, historically based reasons. It may also be true that war has been ubiquitous around the world in both premodern and modern times, but it is important to distinguish between the ubiquity of war in the world and world war, which is a modern phenomenon.

In the same way, the world-system approach to the study of war is geographically defined. It is not a study of war in the world, but of war in the world-system. As it happens, the modern world-system did not always cover the earth. It first emerged as a coherent system in Europe and was slowly globalized—made into a worldwide world-system—through diplomacy, trade, conquest, and war.

In this context, war has three dimensions: war between actors who were part of the emerging, European-based world-system and actors who stood outside it (the wars of conquest and incorporation in the Americas, Africa, and Asia); wars between states within the world-system (Anglo-Dutch, Franco-German, Indo-Pakistani) and among groups of states (Thirty Years' War, Napoleonic Wars, World Wars I and II); and irregular, revolutionary, and civil wars within states (insurgencies in the Philippines, Palestine, and Sri Lanka; American and Spanish civil wars; French and Russian revolutions).

Obviously the distinctions between these three kinds of world-system wars blur easily. British and French states waged war with each other in India during their conquest of the subcontinent; revolutionary war in Vietnam segued into civil and interstate war during its duration of more than thirty years. For the most part, war in the world-system is waged across a spectrum of violence, from individual acts of assassination to the use of nuclear weapons. This underscores the need for an approach that is comprehensive, not based exclusively on war between nation-states, and that appreciates the changing geography of the world-system over time. For instance, World War Alpha, as Wallerstein (1984, 41–42) calls the Thirty Years' War, was conducted in a theater extending from Antwerp to Cartagena and from Cadiz to Bombay. But while it was a nearly worldwide war, the theater was smaller in real terms than subsequent world wars. World War Beta (the Napoleonic Wars) and World War Gamma (World Wars I and II) each dramatically expanded the theater of war and left smaller and smaller areas untouched by combat. Presumably a world war using thermonuclear weapons in large quantities (World War Delta) would leave no part of the world untouched.

Contributors to this volume give considerable attention to world war. Although the discussion of systemwide conflict is crucial to an understanding of conflict in itself, the relation between world war and other, more prevalent forms of war needs to be addressed. It is also important to assess the relative impact of various forms of war on the system as a whole. Do world wars have a greater impact on the development of the system than, say, wars of conquest and incorporation, or the French or Russian revolutions, or the antisystemic rebellions of 1848 and 1968? The answer to this question would put the discussion of world war, and the assumption that it is central to the understanding of war in the world-system, in a wider context.

From a world-system perspective, war is an integral part of the political and economic development of the capitalist world-economy. War is not a political aberration or an economic externality, a radical departure from the normal or peacetime workings of the system. As the historian Frederic Lane (1979, 3) observed, profit and protection—the search for profitable trade and the defense and expansion of trade by force—were intimately linked.

Today it is fashionable to describe the military-industrial complex that provides profit and protection in the United States as a recent development. But similar complexes emerged at the beginning of the modern world-system. Elizabethan trade warriors such as Sir Francis Drake are different in form but not in kind from Grumman Corporation and the U.S. Marines. The chief distinction between early modern and contemporary military-industrial complexes is that a division of labor developed between profit-seeking enterprises and protection-providing states in the period between Sir Francis Drake and Oliver North. In the early modern period, for instance, commercial ships were armed and trade was conducted under the barrels of a ship's own guns. Today in the Persian Gulf, unarmed commercial ships seek profit from trade and states provide the warships to protect that trade, but trade is still conducted under the barrel of a gun.

As profit making and protection providing have been divided between enterprises and states, the relation between political and economic development and war has become more complex and oblique. The relation between political economy and war is the subject of considerable debate, in which the authors of this volume participate.

To analyze this oblique relation, scholars typically study the political-economic development of the system in conjunction with the study of war. As a practical matter, this means using data on the expansion and stagnation of the world-economy, what economists call "long waves," to develop an economic date line on which information about the incidence of war can be set. The juxtaposition of long waves, which periodize economic development, and war, typically measured by the number of battle deaths in a given year (Goldstein 1988), is then used to explain how economic development is related to war.

Two general theories have emerged in this context. Some scholars argue that economic expansion contributes to world war because economic growth provides states with the resources to wage war. Others argue that economic downturns contribute to world war because they stimulate economic and military competition among core states.

While the exploration of these issues is important, the treatment of the relation between economic development and war needs to be broadened. The use of long waves to periodize and describe the vicissitudes of economic development is necessary but insufficient. Long waves, which were used by the Soviet economist Nikolai Kondratieff to describe the roughly fifty-year cycle of expansion and contraction, are not the only temporal structures of the system. Borrowing from French historian Fernand Braudel, Wallerstein (1988) has identified both the *longue durée* (a long-term, more than 150-year period of secular development) and the episodic events of daily life as important temporal features of the world-system.

In addition to long-term secular trends, long-wave cycles, and episodic, short-term developments, it is important to examine war from a nonchronological perspective. Chronological time, which uses clocks and maps to chart the progress of war, is itself a product of the modern world-system and of war (Schaeffer 1982). But chronological time is not the only useful form of time for world-historical research. As Marx said of the past in the *18th Brumaire,* history repeats itself, "the first time as tragedy, the second time as farce" (1975, 15), and of the present, "The social revolution of the 19th century does not draw its poetry from the past, but only from the future" (1975, 18). From this perspective, history can be repetitive, not merely sequential. If one looks at the five Arab-Israeli wars and the three Indo-Pakistani wars in the contemporary period, it is clear that any attempt to explain these wars should take their repetitive character into account.

For Braudel and Wallerstein, long waves are cyclical. Implicit in this conception is the assumption that history does repeat itself in some fashion, that periods of economic expansion or war are like previous periods in important respects. Unfortunately, some scholars who deploy long-wave methodologies in their study of war forget the repetitive character of long waves and use them merely to differentiate between successive epochs. But if the past can be repeated, the study of the history of war has to depart from what Perry Anderson calls "chronological monomism" to explain how and in what ways history is repeated. As Anderson says of absolutist states, "There is no such thing as a uniform temporal medium: for the *times* of the major Absolutisms . . . were precisely enormously diverse. . . . Their *dates* were the same but their *times* were separate" (1974, 10, emphasis added).

The second point that Marx makes is that just as the past can be expressed in the present, the present can be shaped by the future. The threat of global nuclear war, a "core war of the future" as Christopher Chase-Dunn and Kenneth O'Reilly call it, undoubtedly shapes the contemporary world in a dramatic way. The future shapes the development of deterrence ideology and contributes to the deployment of massive, superpower nuclear arsenals. The implication of this perspective for the study of war is that scholars must be alert to the multiple temporal forms in which developments take place.

The treatment of war and the use of data on the number of battle deaths to measure its incidence also need to be broadened. This quantitative measure obscures the relative impact of war in particular settings. For example, during the years between 1971 and 1982, 2,300 people died in the conflict in Northern Ireland and 17,000 were injured—an injury or death for one out of every twenty households. According to Padraig O'Malley, "If you multiply the figures by a factor of 150 to arrive at comparable figures for the U.S. population . . . the number of dead would stand at 345,000—almost as many as the number of people who died in the American Civil War—and the number of civilians injured at 2,550,000" (1983, 10–11). This comparative dimension is necessary if the intensity of war and its impact on different populations are to be explained.

The use of military casualties in battle-death figures also obscures another important development: the changing relation between military and civilian casualties. In World War I, twenty soldiers were killed for every civilian; in World War II, the ratio of military to civilian dead dropped to 1:1; in the Korean War it shifted to 1:5. Rising civilian death tolls are typically blamed on the development of "total war," in which the deployment of new military technologies and the breakdown of social constraints on the use of weapons of mass destruction against civilian populations play an important role.

A cursory glance at the history of wars of conquest and incorporation in the early modern period suggests that military:civilian death ratios were similar to, perhaps worse than, contemporary ratios. It may be that the ratio was initially unfavorable to civilians (recall Cortez's campaigns in the Americas), became increasingly more favorable to civilians as soldiers acquired rules of conduct, and then reversed itself during this century. Alternatively, it may be that wars between European military-industrial complexes and peripheral and Third World people have always been, and continue to be, unfavorable to civilians and that the treatment of European populations in this century's world wars has begun to mimic the treatment of peripheral civilian groups. An exploration of these developments would place the use of battle-death measures in a wider context.

But however the relation between economic development and war is expressed, world-system scholars assume that the pursuit of profit affects the capacity to make war: capitalist development affects the character of war, and war the structure of capitalist development. In this context, it is also important to examine the political economy of war itself, the composition and character of military-industrial complexes. During the seventeenth and eighteenth centuries, for example, Great Britain and France waged a series of maritime wars as part of their contest for political and economic hegemony in the world. Both states worked to develop effective battle fleets that could conclude this long-running conflict on favorable terms. At the beginning of this contest, ships of the line were relatively ineffective instruments of war. Unless one side possessed an overwhelming numerical advantage, it could not inflict a decisive defeat on the other. As Admiral Clowdisley Shovel wrote in the seventeenth century, " 'Tis, without a miracle, number that gains victory" (Bromley and Ryan 1971, 794). Because the Anglo-French arms race resulted in naval parity, they waged inconclusive wars throughout most of this period.

The naval stalemate was broken by several developments. The British deployed a brutally efficient system of impressment to recruit labor into the maritime work force and imposed an increasingly savage discipline on sailors to improve ship handling and increase the rates of fire of battleship fleets (Schaeffer 1984). The transformation of labor relations at sea, together with improved strategies (blockade) and tactics (breaking the enemy's line of battle during combat), increased the effectiveness of British fleets and made it possible to wage decisive battles, which destroyed French fleets and crippled continental French armies.

At the beginning of this period, in 1653, equally matched Dutch and British fleets managed to fight a three-day battle that resulted in the loss of only three Dutch warships. But by the end of this period, in Admiral Horatio Nelson's day, the British navy was able to destroy wholesale enemy fleets, even when they were evenly matched in number, and Nelson could boast: "If we had taken 10 ships out of the enemy's eleven, and let the eleventh escape . . . I would never call such a good day" (Mahan 1918, 185).

The attempt to develop military forces so that they can decisively wage war stimulated the transformation of the means and relations of production. In war, as in business enterprises, the diffusion of technologies and competition among rivals results, over time, in what might be called the falling rate of military effectiveness. This should be understood not as a decrease in the destructiveness of military technologies in absolute terms—these undergo a secular increase—but in relative terms. The development of breech-loading rifles, machine guns, and heavy artillery for a time increased the destructiveness of European military-industrial complexes and made them more effective in wars with non-European peoples (the Boxer Rebellion, for instance), but over time, it decreased the effectiveness of European armies in intra-European war.

The diffusion of military-industrial technologies (not just hardware but also conscription) eventually prevented Europeans from waging decisive campaigns (contrast the Franco-Prussian War, when these technologies were new and un-evenly distributed, to World War I). It was not until they developed tanks and airplanes during the interwar period that Europeans, Americans, and Asians could once again wage war decisively—the blitzkrieg and its combined-operations successors.

Curiously, the development of the atomic bomb, which represented an enormous advance in destructiveness, made it once again difficult for states to wage decisive wars. Atomic and new high-technology weapons, together with the development of new interstate political institutions like the United Nations, contributed to a falling rate of military effectiveness. Military stalemate has been the rule in wars in Korea, Vietnam, the Persian Gulf and Middle East, and the subcontinent. This is true even where superpowers possess tremendous military advantages against peripheral opponents. There have been some exceptions—the Malvinas/Falklands War and the 1967 Arab-Israeli War—but even these decisive military campaigns did not produce decisive political results. In many of these wars, the development of mass-based, ideologically motivated, low-tech guerrilla insurgencies has blunted the effectiveness of high-tech militaries, and the very destructiveness of nuclear weaponry has inhibited its tactical use. At the same time, there has also been a corresponding decline in the effectiveness of guerrilla war as a result of the counterdeployment of irregular forces—death squads and Contras—by states and superpowers. A world-system perspective, which examines the political economy of war in comprehensive and comparative terms, permits the exploration of these developments.

A world-system approach to the study of war also requires the examination of the changing structure of political relations in the interstate system, how war is related to these changes, and how political developments within states contribute to war. In this volume, authors devote a good deal of attention to the general structure of political relations in the interstate system and of the hegemony of states within it.

One feature of the modern world-system that distinguishes it from previous political-economic systems or empires is that no one state rules the system. Instead, political power is multifocal, and a number of competing core states vie for partial power. Occasionally, one state emerges as preeminent and exercises a hegemony over other states in the system. According to Wallerstein, three states—the Netherlands in the seventeenth century, Great Britain in the nineteenth, and the United States in the second half of the twentieth—have been hegemonic, but their hegemony has been qualified in two ways. First, it is temporary. These states exercised political, economic, and military hegemony for only a short time (twenty-five to fifty years). Second, it is partial. They are never able to establish the kind of direct political control over the entire system that was characteristic of the Roman, Mogul, and Chinese empires.

Some states have aspired to establish themselves as heads of global empires—Spain in the sixteenth century, France in the late eighteenth century, and Germany in the mid-twentieth century—but their totalitarian, as opposed to hegemonic, projects were curbed by the weight of states allied against them. These anti-imperial alliances have included states that subsequently emerged as hegemonic, but they were permitted to rule because they were committed to liberal hegemony, not totalitarian dictatorship, in the system.

While the interstate system that emerged in the sixteenth century has been multifocal and characterized by successive balances of power—the Treaty of Westphalia, the Concert of Europe, and the United Nations (Wallerstein 1984, 42)—and oscillates between periods of interstate competition and hegemony, it changes over time. After World War II, for instance, the United States and the Soviet Union together constructed a new interstate system based on independent nation-states to replace the system organized by Great Britain, which was composed of heterogeneous state forms: empires with complex hierarchies (dominions, colonies, protectorates, and mandates), republican nation-states, and dynastic and military regimes. The United States and the Soviet Union created the United Nations as the institutional expression of this new system and advanced self-determination to promote the secession of colonies from European empires and the creation of independent nation-states (Schaeffer 1989).

World war played an important role in this process, breaking up the old British-dominated system and advancing the new U.S.-Soviet system. It is impossible to understand contemporary war without examining the changing political structure of the interstate system as a whole and political development within its constituent nation-states.

Conflict and war within states are important elements in the global spectrum of violence. To understand rebellion and civil war in the world-system, it is important to examine the two forms of violence within states, one ethnic and the other secular (in the sense of "worldly," not "long-term"). In many states, political power is contested by groups defining themselves in ethnic terms. Religion, race, and language are all components of an ethnic identity, which is used to organize political movements that can contest for power. In the contemporary world, this mode of organization and identification defines political struggles in states like Sri Lanka, Ethiopia, Israel, Cyprus, and Northern Ireland. Elsewhere, political power is contested along secular lines. In Poland, the two Koreas, the Philippines, and Nicaragua, for example, economic and political identities define the lines of cleavage.

Although one form tends to dominate in any given state, politics is rarely defined exclusively in ethnic or secular terms. The Polish proletariat promotes Catholic piety; secessionist Tamils advocate class war against Buddhist Sinhalese. The mixture of ethnic and secular politics, which gives rise to civil and interstate war, means that scholars must appreciate the political economy of war in economic and sociological-anthropological terms. Secular, class-based political analyses alone will not suffice. Again, a catholic approach to the study of conflict and war is essential.

If a world-system approach to the study of war is confined to a particular historical period (roughly the 1500s to the present) and geography (an expanding area that eventually incorporated the whole world) and rooted in a particular political economy (that of a capitalist world-economy in which the search for profit and provision of protection are joined), then the authors in this volume contribute to this perspective.

REFERENCES

Anderson, Perry. 1974. *Lineages of the Absolutist State*. London: New Left Books.
Bromley, J. S., and A. N. Ryan. 1971. "Navies." In *The New Cambridge Modern History,* vol. 6, edited by J. S. Bromley. Cambridge: Cambridge University Press.
Goldstein, Joshua. 1988. *Long Cycles: Prosperity and War in the Modern Age*. New Haven: Yale University Press.
Lane, Frederic. 1979. *Profits from Power*. Albany: State University of New York Press.
Mahan, A. T. 1918. *The Influence of Sea Power upon History, 1660–1783*. 12th ed. Boston: Little, Brown.
Mao Tse-tung. 1967. *Selected Military Writings of Mao Tse-tung*. Peking: Foreign Languages Press.
Marx, Karl. 1975. *The 18th Brumaire of Louis Bonaparte*. New York: International Publishers.
O'Malley, Padraig. 1983. *The Uncivil Wars: Ireland Today*. Boston: Houghton Mifflin.
Schaeffer, Robert K. 1982. "The Standardization of Time and Space." In *Ascent and Decline in the World-System,* edited by Edward Friedman, 69–90. Political Economy of the World-System Annuals, vol. 5. Beverly Hills: Sage Publications.
———. 1984. "The Chains of Bondage Broke: The Proletarianization of Seafaring Labor, 1600–1800." Ph.D. diss., State University of New York at Binghamton.
———. 1990. *Warpaths: The Politics of Partition*. New York: Hill and Wang.
Wallerstein, Immanuel. 1984. *The Politics of the World-Economy*. Cambridge: Cambridge University Press.
———. 1988. *The Inventions of TimeSpace Realities: Toward an Understanding of Our Historical Systems*. Binghamton, N.Y.: Fernand Braudel Center.

2

WAR IN THE CORE OF THE WORLD-SYSTEM: TESTING THE GOLDSTEIN THESIS

Terry Boswell, Mike Sweat, and John Brueggemann

Research on the dynamics of the world-system can largely be divided between studies of dependent development during relatively recent periods and long-term historical studies that concentrate on the origins and development of the capitalist system.[1] For the latter, the theoretical and empirical challenge is to establish systemic dynamics that persist throughout the history of world capitalism. While some processes and trends are easily observed in capitalist systems, such as commodification or capital accumulation, evidence of systematic variation at the global level is more difficult to obtain. Historical studies of long-term world dynamics have centered on three principal variables: long waves of extended economic expansion and stagnation, a cycle of hegemony by leading core powers, and reoccurrence of major core wars (Wallerstein 1974, 1980; Frank 1978; Chase-Dunn, 1989).

In an innovative study, Joshua Goldstein (1988) has recently examined extensive long-term quantitative data in order to investigate the relationship between these three dynamics. He joins the long-wave and war/hegemony debates, stating the proposition that the combination of long waves and hegemony determines the conditions that produce a systematic variation in the severity of major core wars. In so doing, he provides a new analysis and data set for examining this frequently asserted proposition in world-system theory.[2] In this chapter, both the logical assumptions of the theory and the empirical evidence of systemic variation are rigorously examined.

The evidence of an association between long waves and war provided by

Goldstein is one of the most extensive and important findings for the long-term study of world-system dynamics. He suggests that long expansion periods lead to more severe wars for two reasons: expansion heightens intracore competition for markets and territory and increases the monetary and aggressive psychological resources necessary to initiate military endeavors (1985, 264). His empirical evidence is not overwhelming, but he finds a clear association between long economic expansion periods and the severity of major intracore wars, measured in terms of average annual fatalities (military or civilian). Fatalities were approximately four times higher during long expansion periods than during stagnation periods (1985, 244–48).[3]

Goldstein's article is frequently cited as evidence of the validity of world-system theory, yet it lacks a rigorous statistical analysis of the data (see Chase-Dunn and O'Reilly, chapter 4 in this volume). Despite the theoretical importance of both long waves and hegemony, Goldstein examines only the former. The long-wave findings may be spurious once data for the cycle of hegemony are introduced. Alternatively, the relationship between hegemony and war described in historical studies may not hold in a model that includes long waves. In addition, Goldstein leaves the causal theory underdeveloped.

There are technical problems with Goldstein's analysis as well. His use of annual average fatalities to measure the severity of wars does not control for the size of the population involved in the war. Two equally severe wars will require radically different amounts of resources if the warring population bases differ widely. Making the severity of war relative to population size is necessary to adequately test the theory. Also, while Goldstein notes that scholars differ over the dating of long waves (1988, 413, 434), he uses the dates most favorable to his thesis.

Though such shortcomings in Goldstein's work must be addressed, his objective of developing a theory of long waves and hegemony that explains the outbreak of major intracore wars is important because existing theories are logically flawed. They do not explain the role of market competition and fail to appreciate the relative autonomy of the state. Analysis of three versions of the long-wave variable while controlling for hegemony in a time-series regression model strongly supports Goldstein's contention that there is an association between long waves and the initiation of intense wars. On the other hand, hegemonic ascent appears to be associated with the level of war intensity but not with the initiation of wars.

MAJOR WARS AND LONG WAVES

Major wars are those between at least two great powers that involve over 50,000 troops (see Levy 1983, 1–19, 47–48, on the definition of great powers; also Wright 1942). Since Wright's pioneering work, which documented the dates and characteristics of major wars, numerous studies have pointed out cyclical and other apparent patterns in their occurrence (Wright 1942; Levy 1983; Small and Singer 1972). The study of international relations abounds with analyses of war, but only recently have scholars begun to incorporate or contest world-system analyses. Bueno de Mesquita (1980) categorizes this research into eight sets of theories, each with an extensive conceptual and empirical literature. The purpose of this study is not to develop a global theory of the causes of war, but to develop a specific world-system theory of the relationship between war, long waves, and hegemony.

Long waves are extended periods of economic expansion and stagnation. Kondratieff ([1926] 1979) is usually cited as the founder of studies on long waves, which are sometimes called "Kondratieffs." Schumpeter (1939) later gave long waves more theoretical coherence. The literature on long waves since Kondratieff and Schumpeter is extensive, and the theory is currently undergoing a revival due to the onset of an extended economic stagnation in the late 1960s (see Barr 1979). Mandel (1975, 1980), Mensch (1979), and Gordon, Edwards, and Reich (1982) have contributed new theoretical developments. The perspective used here is based on a synthesis of recent long-wave theories found in Boswell (1987).[4]

The exact length of a long wave is indeterminate, but each complete wave lasts between fifty and sixty years.[5] The earliest recorded long wave began in 1496, a period of extended stagnation. The current period is part of a downturn that began in 1968. Evidence of long waves prior to the nineteenth century is sketchy at best because it relies mainly on price fluctuations and historical reports of "good" versus "bad" times. Braudel (1972) and Frank (1978) identified long waves prior to the nineteenth century, but they did not explain how waves during agricultural capitalism differ from those produced by industrial capitalism. Mandel's (1975, 1980) evidence of long waves since 1790 is more reliable.

Goldstein combined the various dating schemes to produce a continuous series, outlined in table 2.1. Goldstein (1985, 436–37) also calculated the average annual change in prices over each long-wave period for twenty-six different price indexes from nine different core countries. None of the indexes cover the entire time period, nor does any one series provide a high-quality source of data. On the other hand, the synchronous pattern of prices from divergent sources lends credence to the proposition of a corewide economic wave. An alternative wave variable based on the average of the yearly price changes (column 3) was computed. The alternate price-change variable measures the magnitude of economic change for each long-wave period.

The expansive periods are caused by accumulation innovations (Boswell 1987), a series of technical and social changes in production and marketing that rapidly increase productivity, capital turnover, and profits. Accumulation innovations were developed during the previous stagnation when business and government were forced to experiment with new methods. Expansion is prolonged by a multiplier effect of bunched investment in the initial innovations and by subsequent improvements. During the expansive period, profit rates are relatively high and recessions are light.

Table 2.1
Long Waves and Hegemony, 1496–1968

Economic Long Wave		Price Change	Hegemony	
Period	Type	Percent	Period	Type
1496-	S	2.73	1496-	No Hegemon
1509-	E	2.80		
1529-	S	-2.18		
1539-	E	3.25		
1559-	S	3.28		
1575-	E	2.95	1575-	Ascent (U.N.)
1595-	S	-0.75	1590-	Victory (U.N.)
1621-	E	0.68	1620-	Maturity (U.N.)
1650-	S	-0.59	1650-	Decline (U.N.)
1689-	E	-0.28	1672-	No Hegemon
1720-	S	0.53		
1747-	E	1.09		
1762-	S	0.52		
1790-	E	3.52	1798-	Ascent (U.K.)
1814-	S	-0.55	1815-	Victory (U.K.)
(1826*)				
1848-	E	0.81	1850-	Mature (U.K.)
1872-	S	-1.95	1873-	Decline (U.K.)
1893-	E	2.06	1897-	Ascent (U.S.)
1917-	S	-3.46	1920-	Victory (U.S.)
1940-	E	4.40	1945-	Mature (U.S.)
1968-	S	n.a.	1967-	Decline (U.S.)

Sources: Long Waves: Mandel (1980); Goldstein (1985); Price Change: constructed from Goldstein (1985, appendix I); Hegemony: Hopkins and Wallerstein (1979).

a. Price Changes are the percent annual average change during the period. The variable is an average of price changes in all twenty-six price series for nine core countries found in Goldstein (1985, 436–37).

b. E = Expansion period; S = Stagnation period.

c. Based on price series, Kondratieff ([1926] 1979) divided the long wave starting in 1790 at 1813. The high point in prices occurs around 1813 due to the Napoleonic Wars. Mandel divides the long wave at 1825–1826 based on production data for Britain. Goldstein uses Kondratieff's dates.

Expansive periods are followed by a period of stagnation in which profit rates decline, recessions are steep and prolonged, and capital accumulation is hindered by sluggish demand and cautious investment. Stagnation periods are caused by the exhaustion and saturation of the accumulation innovations. A general crisis develops when the length and intensity of stagnation indicate that expansive growth will not automatically reoccur and that institutional and political solutions are necessary to create conditions for renewed expansion. Experimentation ensues until the next accumulation innovation restores expansion.

Because the capitalist world market and the international division of labor integrate national economies into a single system, long waves are roughly synchronized as a single global phenomenon. Each wave in the world-economy presents roughly similar economic conditions for every core state. Goldstein's argument does not fully explain why expansion is empirically associated with war, since his principal goal is to confirm the empirical existence of long waves and their association with major wars, but he suggests that an expansionary upswing will lead to war because it could (1) "heighten competition for markets, resources and strategic territory"; (2) "support higher military expenditures, arms races, and the costs of war"; and (3) "create an aggressive, expansionist psychological mood" (1988:261–64).

Of his three propositions, the first is the weakest. Although an intensification of market competition may increase pressure on the state to use its military resources in order to gain privileged access to resources, there is no reason to believe that competition is greater when economies are expanding than when they are stagnating. On the contrary, states may initiate war in attempting a political solution to the general crisis of an extended stagnation (Lenin [1917] 1939; Lotta 1984; Frank 1982; Bergesen 1985). The economic crisis theory is also flawed because it only explains why an imperialist core state would seek to control peripheral markets, not other core states (Boswell, forthcoming). Intracore war may follow a crisis, but only if conflict results from the struggle over control of the periphery rather than from internal economic stagnation.

The military and psychological theories are both more logically consistent and better supported by the empirical evidence. The two are interdependent and might better be considered a resource theory of war. A resource theory predicts war whenever states have sufficient military and psychological (or ideological) resources to make it viable. The empirical findings correspond more closely with the resource theory. Goldstein found an association only between economic expansions and the severity of wars (that is, number of annual battle deaths). No clear association existed between long waves and the number of length of wars. This means that economic expansion produces the resources for larger and more deadly wars, but not more of them. Additional evidence comes from the timing and reciprocal effects of war. Thompson and Zuk (1982) found that wars are more likely to begin near the end of an expansion, when resources are greatest. When undertaking a major war, the participants exhaust their resources and inflate their currency, which tends to inaugurate a long stagnation period.

While better supported, the resource theory assumes that states make war whenever they can afford it. Kiser (chapter 5 in this volume) argues that this assumption applies only to states with highly autonomous rulers who benefit from war, and rarely, if ever, to the rest of the states. Any variation in the autonomy of rulers would greatly affect the accumulation and use of military resources. The decline in autonomy over time due to democratization could account for the decreasing frequency of major wars. On the other hand, the capture of the state by militarist or imperialist political movements (such as the Nazis) can explain why military resources are accumulated and wars begun despite long stagnations. This would explain the major anomaly in the theory, World War II, which followed a military buildup during a period of stagnation (but not at the depths of a depression as an economic crisis theory of war would predict).[6]

Resource theory thus has a hidden assumption that core states are highly autonomous. But the example of the Nazis also points out that one great power is required to initiate a major war. The rest have no choice but to react. It is only necessary to assume that a single great power has a ruler (or ruling political movement) who benefits from war and has the autonomy to initiate it. This not only makes the theory more plausible, but is important for the empirical analysis, since it is difficult to measure state autonomy.

MAJOR WARS AND THE CYCLE OF HEGEMONY

A hegemonic power is one with substantial economic superiority that penetrates the world market to such an extent that injuries to the hegemon have negative consequences for the world economy as a whole. The Netherlands, the United Kingdom, and the United States have been widely recognized as hegemons (see table 2.1). Given the unequal and uneven development of the world capitalist economy, it is not surprising to find a single core power with a superior position vis-à-vis competing core powers. What is more difficult to recognize, because it occurs slowly over centuries, is the rhythmic succession of hegemons identified by Hopkins and Wallerstein (1979), Modelski (1987), and others (see Chase-Dunn, 1989).

According to Wallerstein (1974), hegemons gain their position by first obtaining a substantial advantage in labor productivity (first in agriculture, then in industry). High productivity leads to the international marketing advantage of lower prices, but equally high (or higher) profits. Military strength and war, which open markets, benefit the hegemon during its ascension. Over time, the higher relative profits produce and attract capital for investment, making the hegemon the world's financial hub.

The loss of hegemony follows a reverse pattern. Higher demand in the world market means that labor costs in the hegemon eventually increase relative to its competitors (although higher productivity rates forestall immediate decline). Outward flows of capital occur when the internal investment market is saturated, that is, when capital concentration coupled with high labor costs makes investment in new versions of existing production unprofitable. As a result, the hegemon eventually loses its productivity advantage to competitors with newer equipment and lower labor costs. The loss of market advantages follows. Military adventures and wars can no longer be easily financed, and they become a drag on growth. The concentration of financial power in the hegemon is the last to disappear as the source of its revenue increasingly consists of internal debt and foreign investment. A fiscal crisis is a clear indicator of hegemonic decline.

The cycle of hegemony can be divided into four phases: hegemonic ascent, when aspirants contend for economic and military advantage; hegemonic victory, when one state clearly emerges as the dominant hegemon; mature hegemony, when the hegemon consolidates its position; and hegemonic decline, when it begins to lose its relative advantage. International market and military competition tends to result in a repeating cycle of hegemony. However, there is no guarantee that a new hegemon will arise, and long periods of relative equality may separate one hegemony from the next.

Väyrynen (1983) argues that the hegemonic ascent period should have the highest association with war. During this period, war is caused by succession struggles among hegemonic aspirants. Core powers are not competing for hegemony during the other three periods.

Chase-Dunn and Rubinson (1977), on the other hand, divide the cycle into two periods: a unicentric period when a single core power is dominant (hegemonic victory and maturity) and a multicentric period when the hegemon is either declining or contenders are ascending. They argue that fewer wars should occur during the unicentric period because the hegemon maintains an overwhelming military advantage and imposes free trade on the world economy. The multicentric period should be associated with greater warfare as the relative power of core states becomes equalized.

In sum, the propositions concerning major wars based on world-system theory are that larger wars occur during long-wave expansions and during multicentric periods in the cycle of hegemony, especially hegemonic ascent. Unicentric periods are associated with peace. Expansion leads to severe wars near its conclusion because military resources are built up, assuming that there is at least one aggressive great power. Multicentric periods lead to war due to competition for succession, while the disparity of power reduces warfare during unicentric periods.

VARIABLES AND METHODS

Goldstein's study covers the years 1496 to 1974, making it one of the few quantitative studies covering nearly the entire history of the capitalist world-system (but see Bergesen and Schoenberg 1980; McGowan 1985; Kiser and Drass 1987; Boswell, forthcoming). The temporal range of his study appears to be determined by the availability of the war and long-wave data and by the theoretical argument that it is the vagaries of the world capitalist economy that predict war.

But should the period prior to 1640 be included (Boswell, forthcoming)? This period is part of the transition to capitalism during the "long sixteenth century" of 1450–1640, and neither the integration of the world market not the international capitalist division of labor is solidified until near the end of the period (Wallerstein 1974). However, for the purpose of replicating and testing Goldstein's thesis in this study, we use his dates with one minor exception: the analysis ends in 1967 rather than 1974. The stagnation that began in 1968 has yet to conclude, and it is unknown what wars may yet occur (which would likely have a huge fatality rate). By including the corewide peace since 1968, Goldstein inflates the association of war and expansion without complete evidence. Excluding the last period makes for a more stringent test of the theory.

War

Goldstein (1985, 248–49) concluded that only the severity of wars in terms of average annual fatalities was significantly associated with economic long waves. The severity variable he used (derived from Levy 1983, 83–91) fails to control for the size of the population involved. Fortunately, Levy also provides a variable (called war intensity) that is a ratio of average annual battle fatalities from great-power wars to the total European population at the beginning of the war (235). This variable can be logged to reduce extreme variations, especially troublesome with World War I and World War II (as Goldstein did in a graph but not in his tables, 1985, 247, 250). Using the logged intensity variable provides both a more precise and a more rigorous analysis.

Economic Long Waves

Two long-wave variables can be derived from table 2.1: one that only compares expansion versus stagnation, and a second that includes the magnitude of price changes (see the appendix for codes). Both are expected to have a positive effect on war intensity. However, dating long waves by price changes unfortunately leaves the variable sensitive to sources of inflation other than the increased demand of a prosperous population. Production or distribution bottlenecks, currency speculation, and crop failures can lead to inflation during otherwise stagnant economic periods (such as the stagflation of the late 1970s). As Goldstein points out, Keynesian economic intervention by central governments makes price data suspect after 1930–1945. Using production statistics (usually gross national product) avoids this problem, but data are not available prior to the nineteenth century.

Prior to 1945, price and production dating schemes are nearly identical except for the period 1814–1825. Prices drop off dramatically in 1814, while production remains relatively robust until 1825. Goldstein uses Kondratieff's price-based dates, which have a long stagnation beginning in 1814, rather than Mandel's production-based dates, which continue the expansion until 1825. Yet the drop in prices is likely due more to the end of the British blockade of Napoleonic France than to structural changes in the economy. Leaving out the relatively peaceful years 1815–1825 also increases the association between war and expansion by concentrating the expansion period around the Napoleonic Wars. In order to test whether Goldstein's findings are overly reliant on this disputed dating, a second comparative wave variable based on Mandel's dates was created. Except for the fact that the 1814–1825 period is considered an expansion period, this second wave variable is identical to the first. Mandel's wave variable is also expected to have a positive effect on war, although to a lesser extent. More details and technical information regarding these three variables are given in the Appendix.

Hegemony

Four variables based on phases in the cycle of hegemony were derived from Hopkins and Wallerstein (1979) (see table 2.1 and the Appendix). The phases are hegemonic ascent, hegemonic victory, hegemonic maturity, and hegemonic decline. Periods with no hegemon are the excluded category. Although similar variables have been used elsewhere (Kiser and Drass, 1987; Boswell, forthcoming), these are admittedly crude measures whose length (twenty to forty years) adds to their imprecision. The hegemonic victory and maturity phases are expected to have a negative effect on war intensity, while the hegemonic decline and ascent phases are expected to have a positive effect.

RESULTS

The regression results are summarized here; a full explanation of the equations can be found in the Appendix. Analyses were completed on change and level models of war intensity along with three different measures of long waves. The change model predicts the initiation or termination of war given the previous year by including a lagged dependent variable (which also takes into account the potential linear effects of war; Hicks 1984; Kiser and Drass 1987; Johnston 1972). The magnitude of the change is equal to the annual average intensity of the war—a positive number for the initiation of the war and an equal but negative number for the termination of the war. In this model, Goldstein's version of the long-wave variable retained a statistically significant positive effect on war intensity despite controlling for hegemony and eliminating the post–1968 peace. However, none of the hegemony variables were significant predictors.

A model without the lagged dependent variable was also examined for purposes of comparison. This model predicts the level of war intensity rather than the change in war and peace. The analyses yielded two differences: first, hegemonic maturity, while insignificant in the change model, had a significantly negative effect on war in this equation. Second, Goldstein's long-wave variable dropped to a barely significant level.

Finally, the two alternative long-wave variables were examined using the change model. Surprisingly, the price-change version had no significant effect on war intensity (see the Appendix for discussion). A model using Mandel's production dates of 1826–1848 rather than Goldstein's dates of 1814–1848 produced only slightly different results. This means that the theory is not reliant on the disputed dates.

It appears that the relationship between long waves and change in war, what we have called the "Goldstein thesis," holds under a more rigorous statistical scrutiny that includes the effects of hegemony. The relationship is not dependent on a disputed period where price and production theories of long waves diverge, nor does use of a more theoretically pertinent dependent variable affect the findings.[7]

Only the synthetic price measurement of the magnitude of long waves failed to affect war intensity. One would have expected that the magnitude of economic change would have relevant effects independent of the period effects of waves. It may be that taking the simple average of twenty-six price series from nine countries is inappropriate prior to 1750 because more weight should be given to the hegemonic power or because the world market was not highly integrated in all series. While further refinement and research are needed, the difference between the magnitude and the dummy variables casts some doubt on Goldstein's dating and evidence for long waves during the first half of world capitalism's existence. Future research might break the analysis into different time periods corresponding to the development of capitalism: a period of transition to capitalism lasting from 1496 to 1640; the period of agricultural capitalism, 1640 to 1790; and a period of industrial capitalism from 1790 to the present (see Goldstein 1988, 242–43).

There is also an important difference between the change and level versions of the analyses. Given the previous year's conditions, the long-wave variable has a clearly significant effect on change in war intensity, but only reaches a marginally acceptable level of significance when one examines the level of war intensity. On the other hand, hegemonic maturity, which is insignificant in the change model, reaches significance when one observes the level of war intensity.

Expansive long waves appear to be associated mainly with initiation of the more intense wars and stagnation with their termination. Such a finding is consistent with the resource theory, which argues that states build up their military capabilities and psychological readiness during economic expansions, and that this results in highly intense war. War exhausts the economy of the participants, terminating the expansion. Crisis theories that expect war during the depths of stagnation are not supported. Previous research has indicated that stagnation is associated with core imperialism against the periphery (Boswell, forthcoming), and our initial impression is that crisis theories have overgeneralized from core-periphery wars to intracore wars.

The notable exception is World War II. Goldstein proposes to resolve the problem by considering World Wars I and II a single war because the outcome of World War I was unresolved until the end of World War II (1988, 242–43).[8] Although this is a viable proposition in terms of hegemony (Modelski 1987), it does not answer the question pertinent to a resource theory of war: what led to a military buildup despite the stagnation of the 1930s? A possible political cause of the unexpected war preparations is the (unmeasured) intervening variable of high state autonomy, resulting from fascism in this case. Although difficult to measure, an intervening variable of state autonomy is entirely consistent with the theory once its logical assumptions are examined and elaborated, and it should be considered in future research. In addition, the decline in the frequency of war over time may be due to the long-term decreasing autonomy of the state because of democratization, despite the periodic reversals produced by militarist-imperialist movements.

World War II is also an anomaly because it does not terminate the expansion but is instead followed by the biggest expansion ever in world-system history. One possible reason for this anomaly is the effect of U.S. economic hegemony, which reached maturity after the war. The United States used its hegemonic position to restore the obviously exhausted European and Asian economies. Stagnation would likely have resumed otherwise. Stagnation was avoided because the hegemon largely avoided the devastation of the war. This interpretation of hegemony is unique to U.S. hegemony, which suggests that further research is needed on the general theory of hegemony.

On the other hand, the finding of a lower level (but not change) of war intensity occurring during hegemonic maturity periods is as expected. These are periods when a clear hegemon holds sway over potential contenders. The other three hegemony periods appear to have no effect on either the change or level of war intensity net of the long-wave and time-trend variables. However, dummy coding is a crude measure of hegemony, and the findings may not survive future analysis if higher-quality data can be collected. There are also several versions of the hegemony variables, such as Modelski's theory of long cycles of world leadership (1987), that could be investigated.

A final implication of this study concerns the possibility of an intense intracore war in the future. Characteristics unique to the current period, such as the development of nuclear weapons and the improvement in communication technology, could mitigate against the careless initiation of another world war. But one could have said the same about mustard gas and telephones in the 1920s. A mechanistic interpretation of the analysis would predict the probability of another highly intense war to peak around 2010–2020. This assumes about twenty to thirty years of economic expansion expected to begin in the early 1990s and a concurrent competition for hegemonic ascension by the leading core states.

Of course, mechanistic interpretations assume a false determinacy about human history. The association between economic expansion and the intensity of war depends on the accumulation of resources by the militaries of the contending nations. On the one hand, militarist or neo-imperialist political movements can sever this association, as evidenced by the military buildup in Germany during the late 1930s and in the United States in the early 1980s. The reality of the latter buildup vitiates the immediate need for a long expansion, bringing closer the possibility of war. On the other hand, a renewed worldwide antiwar movement, such as was briefly seen in the late 1960s and early 1980s, could reduce both military spending and state autonomy, severing the relationship in the opposite direction. However, peace movements by themselves are constrained to temporary success by the dynamics of the world-system, which cyclically reassert hegemonic competition. Only a fundamental change to a less competitive world-system will make peace a lasting proposition.

NOTES

1. Presented at the 12th Annual Political Economy of the World-System Conference, "War and Revolution in the World-System," Emory University, Atlanta, Georgia, March 24–26 1988. The authors would like to thank Al Bergesen, Randy Blazak, Christopher Chase-Dunn, Joshua Goldstein, and Alex Hicks for their helpful suggestions.

2. Goldstein (1988) provides an extensive review of the literature on long waves, hegemony, and war. Chase-Dunn (1987, 1989) provides a more critical analysis of the theories. See also chapters in this volume by Chase-Dunn, Kiser, and Väyrynen and other new work by Modelski (1987), Goldfrank (1987), and Bergesen (1985).

3. Prior research by Thompson and Zuk (1982) also found an association between long waves and war using an ARIMA model that did not include hegemony and covered a much shorter period (1816 to 1914). However, they suggest that without war-induced inflation, long waves measured only by prices would be nearly inperceptible (634). On the other hand, they also find that most expansion periods begin prior to war. Goldstein acknowledges (1985, 428–30, 441 n. 36) the problem of bidirectional causality, but claims that the evidence is insufficient to reach a final conclusion and seems to suggest a bidirectional causality. Our study does not allow us to resolve this issue, but we mitigate the possibility of reverse causality in two ways. First, the long-wave variable is lagged one year in all models. This creates a temporal difference between waves and war, although the length of waves results in substantial overlap. Second, we examine the initiation and termination of war as discrete events, thereby excluding an association of long waves with the high inflation occurring during the war. Despite these attempts to mitigate against it, reverse causality cannot be dismissed entirely.

4. The evidence and theory of long waves have been developed only for the core of the world economy and may differ outside it. Long waves in the periphery are not pertinent for this study but are an obvious area for future research.

5. Long waves must be distinguished from business cycles, which are periodic recessions and recoveries that occur about every seven to eleven years. Long waves encompass but do not cause business cycles. Instead, long waves structure the economic environment in which the shorter cycles take place. Business cycles have an internal causal dynamic based upon the rhythm of the market in a capitalist economy. Long expansions or stagnations affect the buoyancy of both supply and demand in the business cycle.

6. Although both Goldstein and Mandel date the upswing beginning in 1939, the trough of the depression occurred in 1932–1933. The core had been growing for five to six years before the outbreak of war (1938 was recessionary year). Also, the Soviet Union, whose battle losses contributed most to the intensity of the war, had been growing rapidly since 1925.

7. The choice of war intensity over severity was made on *a priori* theoretical grounds.

While we consider the former a better variable, for purposes of comparison, we also ran the analysis with log war severity for the change model in column one of table 2.2 and found similar results: SEVERITY = 8.579 + 0.720 LAGSEVERITY + 0.888 LAGWAVE + 0.278 LAGHASC − 0.294 LAGHVIC − 0.387 LAGHMAT − 0.108 LAGHDEC − 0.004 YEAR (understandardized coefficients; r^2 = .678). As in the comparable equation for log war intensity, only the lagged dependent, long wave and year variables are significant.

8. Goldstein (1985, 427–31) also suggests that post–1945 wars might not show the expected relationship with waves because of permanent government intervention in the economy starting in World War II.

REFERENCES

Barr, Kenneth. 1979. "Long Waves: A Selected Annotated Bibliography." *Review* 2:671–718.

Bergensen, Albert. 1985. "Cycles of War in the Reproduction of the World Economy." In *Rhythms in Politics and Economics,* edited by Paul M. Johnson and William R. Thompson, 313–31. New York: Praeger.

Bergensen, Albert, and Ronald Schoenberg. 1980. "Long Waves of Colonial Expansion and Contraction, 1415–1969." In *Studies of the Modern World-System,* edited by Albert Bergensen, 231–277. New York: Academic Press.

Boswell, Terry. 1987. "Accumulation Innovations in the American Economy: The Affinity for Japanese Solutions to the Current Crisis." In *America's Changing Role in the World-System,* edited by Terry Boswell and Albert Bergensen, 95–126. New York: Praeger.

———. Forthcoming. "Colonial Empires and the Capitalist World-System: A Quantitative Analysis of Colonization, 1650–1960." *American Sociological Review.*

Braudel, Fernand. 1972. *The Mediterranean and the Mediterranean World in the Age of Philip II.* Vol. 1. London: Collins.

Bueno de Mesquita, Bruce. 1980. "Theories of International Conflict: An Analysis and Appraisal." In *Handbook of Political Conflict,* edited by Ted Robert Gurr, 361–98. New York: Free Press.

Chase-Dunn, Christopher. 1987. "Cycles, Trends, or Transformation? The World-System since 1945." In *America's Changing Role in the World-System,* edited by Terry Boswell and Albert Bergesen, 57–84. New York: Praeger.

———. 1989. *Global Formation: Structures of the World-Economy.* New York: Basil Blackwell.

Chase-Dunn, Christopher, and Richard Rubinson. 1977. "Toward a Structural Perspective on the World-System." *Political and Society* 7:453–76.

Frank, Andre Gunder. 1978. *World Accumulation, 1492–1789.* London: Macmillan.

———. 1982. "Crisis of Ideology and Ideology of Crisis." In S. Amin et al., *Dynamics of Global Crisis,* 109–66. New York: Monthly Review Press.

Goldfrank, Walter L. 1987. "Socialism or Barbarism? The Long-run Fate of the Capitalist World-Economy." In *America's Changing Role in the World-System,* edited by Terry Boswell and Albert Bergesen, 85–92. New York: Praeger.

Goldstein, Joshua. 1985. "Kondratieff Waves as War Cycles." *International Studies Quarterly* 29:411–44.

————. 1988. *Long Cycles: Prosperity and War in the Modern Age*. New Haven: Yale University Press.

Gordon, David, Richard Edwards, and Michael Reich. 1982. *Segmented Work, Divided Workers*. Cambridge: Cambridge University Press.

Hicks, Alexander. 1984. "Elections, Keynes, Bureaucracy, and Class: Explaining U.S. Budget Deficits, 1961–1978." *American Sociological Review* 49:165–82.

Hopkins, Terence, and Immanuel Wallerstein. 1979. "Cyclical Rhythms and Secular Trends of the Capitalist World-Economy: Some Premises, Hypotheses and Questions." *Review* 2:483–500.

Jacobs, David. 1988. "Corporate Economic Power and the State: A Longitudinal Assessment of Two Explanations." *American Journal of Sociology* 93:852–81.

Johnston, J. 1972. *Econometric Models*. 2d ed. New York: McGraw-Hill.

Kiser, Edgar, and Kriss A. Drass. 1987. "Changes in the Core of the World-System and the Production of Utopian Literature in Great Britain and the United States, 1883–1975." *American Sociological Review* 52:286–93.

Kondratieff, Nicholas D. [1926] 1979. "Die langen Wellen der Konjunktur." *Review* 2:519–62.

Lenin, Vladimir I. [1917] 1939. *Imperialism, the Highest Stage of Capitalism*. New York: International Publishers.

Levy, Jack S. 1983. *War in the Modern Great Power System, 1495–1975*. Lexington: University Press of Kentucky.

Lotta, Raymond. 1984. *America in Decline: An Analysis of the Developments toward War and Revolution in the U.S. and Worldwide in the 1980's*. Chicago: Banner Press.

McGowan, Pat. 1985. "Pitfalls and Promise in the Quantitative Study of the World-System: A Reanalysis of Bergesen and Schoenberg's 'Long Waves' of Colonialism." *Review* 8:477–500.

Mandel, E. 1975. *Late Capitalism*. London: New Left Books.

————. 1980. *Long Waves of Capitalist Development: The Marxist Interpretation*. Cambridge: Cambridge University Press.

Mensch, Gerhard. 1979. *Stalemate in Technology: Innovations Overcome the Depression*. Cambridge, Mass.: Ballinger.

Modelski, George, ed. 1987. *Exploring Long Cycles*. Boulder: Lynne Rienner.

Schumpeter, Joseph A. 1939. *Business Cycles*. New York: McGraw-Hill.

Small, Melvin, and J. David Singer. 1972. *Resort to Arms: International and Civil Wars, 1816–1980*. Beverly Hills: Sage Publications.

Thompson, William R., and Gary Zuk. 1982. "War, Inflation, and the Kondratieff Long Wave." *Journal of Conflict Resolution* 26:621–44.

Väyrynen, Raimo. 1983. "Economic Cycles, Power Transitions, Political Management, and Wars between Major Powers." *International Studies Quarterly* 27:389–418.

Wallerstein, Immanuel. 1974. *The Modern World-System*. Vol. 1. New York: Academic Press.

————. 1980. *The Modern World-System*. Vol. 2. New York: Academic Press.

White, Kenneth J. 1978. "A General Computer Program for Econometric Methods— SHAZAM." *Econometrica*:239–40.

Wright, Quincey. 1942. *A Study of War*. Chicago: University of Chicago Press.

APPENDIX: REGRESSION ANALYSIS

The regression equations were estimated using a time-series model that corrects for first-order autocorrelation of errors by means of generalized differences (White 1978). The regression models were performed using the SHAZAM econometrics computer program. The long-wave and three hegemony variables were lagged one year to reflect the time lag between their occurrence and the responses of core states. The lagging also mitigates against reverse causality. Only a one-year lag is used in order to minimize any overlap between different long-wave and hegemony periods. A time-trend variable (YEAR), measured simply by the years 1495 to 1967, was also added to the equation to eliminate any unmeasured effects and reduce the possibility of any spurious effects of linear trending (McGowan 1985, 490; Jacobs 1988, 863).

In the first equation, 2.1, presented in table 2.2, the long-wave, three hegemony, time-trend, and lagged dependent variables are examined for the time range 1496 to 1967. This will be referred to as the change model since it includes the lagged dependent variable. The equation produces a moderately large R^2 (.68), which is common with the inclusion of a lagged dependent variable. The model is devoid of first-order autocorrelation error, indicated by the low Durbin's h statistic ($-.166$).

As expected, there is a significantly positive coefficient for the long-wave variable (.582, $p < .025$, one-tailed test). None of the hegemony variables produced significant coefficients, although the hegemonic maturity variable (LAGHMAT) produced a negative coefficient, and the hegemonic decline (LAGHDEC) and ascent variables (LAGHASC) produced positive coefficients, as was hypothesized. The time-trend variable (YEAR) reached significance with a negative effect, indicating the decline in war over time.

By turning to equation 2.2 of table 2.2, the change model can be compared with a level model. The second equation has a similar R^2 despite lacking a lagged dependent variable because of the correction for autocorrelation in the errors. Note that the rho is exceedingly high (.79). While not changing much in size, the coefficient for the long-wave variable drops to the .10 level of significance (one-tailed test; .20 in a two-tailed test). Because the sign is still in the correct direction and the data are a rough population rather than a sample, this low level of significance is reasonably acceptable.

Hegemonic maturity has a significantly negative effect in this model. Hegemonic ascent also has a much stronger positive effect, although still not significant. Neither of the other hegemony variables showed as much change. As in the prDnegative relationship.

The negative effect of hegemonic maturity on the level but not the change in war intensity is probably due to the difference in the way the models are constructed rather than to theoretical differences. A phase of hegemony encompasses a longer time period than that of most wars. Since a war is both initiated and terminated during the time of a maturity phase, the association will cancel out in the change model even though the level of war intensity for all years is significantly lower. The level model thus exposes a significant association that was hidden by a statistical artifact of the change model and the crude measurement of hegemony.

Using only the change model in table 2.3 (that is, including the lagged dependent variable), the two alternative wave variables are examined. The first equation, 3.1, substitutes the price-change version of long waves. Surprisingly, it has no significant effect on the change in war intensity. Both the dummy coded wave variable from equation

Table 2.2
Regression Analyses of Log War Intensity on Long Wave, Hegemony, and Time Trend Variables: 1496–1967

	Dependent Variable: Log War Intensity (WARINT)	
Independent Variables	2.1 b	2.2 b
Long Waves (LAGWAVE t-1)	.582*	.571***
Hegemonic Ascent (LAGHASC t-1)	.049	.922
Hegemonic Victory (LAGHVIC t-1)	-.059	-.357
Mature Hegemony (LAGHMAT t-1)	-.245	-1.234***
Hegemonic Decline (LAGHDEC t-1)	.016	-.593
Time Trend (YEAR)	-.002*	-.007*
Lag Dep. Variable (LWARINT t-1)	.735*	n.a
Constant	4.124*	15.584*
R^2	.682	.679
Adjusted R^2	.677	.676
Durbin-Watson	2.005	1.941
Durbin's h	-.166	n.a.
rho	.068	.787

*p < .025 (t > 1.960) one tailed test
**p < .050 (t > 1.645)
***p < .100 (t > 1.282)

Note: The analysis was corrected for first order autocorrelation (AR1)

Table 2.3

Alternative Long Wave variables in a regression analysis of Log War Intensity on Long Wave, Hegemony, and Time Trend Variables: 1496–1967

	Dependent Variable: Log War Intensity (WARINT)	
Independent Variables	a 3.1 b	b 3.2 b
Long Waves (LAGWAVE t-1)	1.923	.414*
Hegemonic Ascent (LAGHASC t-1)	.260	.166
Hegemonic Victory (LAGHVIC t-1)	-.183	-.152
Mature Hegemony (LAGHMAT t-1)	.046	-.152
Hegemonic Decline (LAGHDEC t-1)	-.133	-.035
Time Trend (YEAR)	-.002*	-.002*
Lag Dep. Variable (LWARINT t-1)	.752*	.739*
Constant	4.189*	4.236*
R2	.677	.679
Adjusted R2	.672	.675
Durbin-Watson	2.004	2.005
Durbin's h	-.116	-.188
rho	.064	.072

```
 *p < .025 (t > 1.960) one tailed test
 **p < .050 (t > 1.645)
***p < .100 (t > 1.282)
```

Note: The analysis was corrected for first order autocorrelation (AR1).

a. An alternative long wave variable based on an index of average price changes is used in equation 3.1 (listed in table 2.1).
b. An alternative dummy coded long wave variable is used in equation 3.2, based on Mandel's dates (that is, 1814-1825=1, see table 2.1).

2.1 (LAGWAVE) and this price-change version are displayed in table 2.1. A close comparison shows that the expected variation in prices prior to 1747 is frequently either nonexistent or even in the wrong direction. Specifically, the change in prices is in the wrong direction for three periods (1539–1558, 1559–1574, 1720–1746). In addition, a difference of less than 0.10 exists between the first two periods (1496–1508 and 1509–1528) and between the fourth and fifth (1539–1558 and 1559–1574). As a result of these differences, the concept of a period that influences the worldview of political actors is not consistent between the two variables prior to about 1750. This inconsistency is apparently sufficient to significantly diminish the effect of the price magnitude variable.

The second model in table 2.3 (3.2) includes Mandel's dating of the dummy coded wave variable for the 1814–1825 period. The coefficient for the wave variable is still significant and only a slightly lower than in the first equation in table 2.2, indicating that the theory is not overly dependent on a disputed definition of waves. As in equation 2.1, none of the hegemony variables reached significance in these change models, but the time-trend variable had the same significant negative effect. A Cook's D test of the possibility that single years were unduly influential was performed for each of the residuals in all of the models. No case has a significant undue influence, the closest being 1919 ($D = .137, F = .998$).

3

The World-System, Militarization, and National Development

Byron L. Davis, Edward L. Kick, and David Kiefer

World-system and dependency writers have exhaustively studied global economic dynamics (trade, investment, and debt) and their determining role in national economic processes (domestic product and inequality).[1] The preponderant concern with world-economic antecedents and national economic outcomes has been fortunate in at least two respects. It has provided a theoretical consistency in the world system literature, and it is in harmony with long-standing intellectual and ideological traditions (Marxism and Leninism). Nonetheless, the economic focus of world-system and dependency writers has restricted their concern with non-economic global links and peripheralized the study of noneconomic, national-level processes. World-system theory has come to be understood as world- and national-economy theory.

International war and domestic revolution have now surfaced as important topics for treatment by world-system and dependency scholars. The scope of the world-system approach correspondingly has been broadened. The need for a structural and sociological approach that recognizes the importance of the multiple forms and outcomes of international linkages also has become more pressing.[2]

The relationships between world-system structure (with its multiple economic and noneconomic components), national conflict, interstate war, militarization, and national development are the primary focus of this chapter. It is important to explain the relationships between militarization and development in Third World countries, a topic that has been neglected in the world-system and dependency literature.[3] Consider that (a) military spending for the world was an estimated $921 billion in 1986 (Stockholm International Peace Research Institute [SIPRI] 1986, 1); (b) the world's armed forces number 30 million, of whom 60 percent serve in the developing world (SIPRI 1987, 4); (c) world arms imports for 1986 were $34.6 billion, with 75 percent destined for the developing world; and (d) thirty-six non-Communist Third World countries are now involved in the production of conventional weapons—a figure double that of the early 1970s.

Scholarly opinion concerning the effects of militarization on development is divided. Modernization theorists have argued that militarization helps Third World development by fostering modernizing attitudes as well as the physical infrastructure required for economic advances. By contrast, the world-system and dependency theorists who examine militarization contend that armed conflict and militarization in the Third World are inherent in the post–1945 world-system, and that they contribute greatly to the economic and political underdevelopment of the Third World.

After these two contending approaches to national development have been summarized, it is possible to test the competing hypotheses with ordinary least squares regression analyses. The test examines the impact of several forms of militarization on economic and political development for a sample representing the entire world and a subsample representing Third World countries only. The results mainly support a modified world-system perspective.

WORLD-SYSTEM AND DEPENDENCY THEORY

World-system and dependency studies emphasize the simultaneous underdevelopment of the Third World and the prosperity of the First and Second worlds. These different patterns of development are seen as a consequence of the economic exploitation of peripheral countries by core countries (Frank 1967, 1980; Galtung 1971; Wallerstein 1974; Chirot 1977). One mechanism of exploitation is the high rate of profit earned overseas by core investors who benefit from monopolistic power. Other mechanisms include debt dependency and the unequal terms of trade between peripheral, semiperipheral, semicore, and core countries (Chase-Dunn 1975). Still another mechanism is the concentrated production of primary products for export in the Third World producers and resulting weaknesses in national infrastructures (Chase-Dunn 1975; Rubinson 1976; Bornschier, Chase-Dunn, and Rubinson 1978; Evans and Timberlake 1980; Bornschier 1981; Stokes and Jaffee, 1982). Taken together, the external relations of Third World countries and the modes of internal production that are associated with them result in the relative stagnation of Third World economies.

Economic stagnation in the Third World perpetuates income differences between elites and masses and encourages a zero-sum competition between the rich and poor over limited resources. The visibility of unattainable elite lifestyles and the structural dislocations associated with the continued intrusion of market forces further heighten discontent among Third World populations (Wolf 1969;

Chirot 1977). Elites attempt to control discontent by imposing military regimes that enforce social and economic inequality. These actions often have exacerbated domestic contention, leading to revolutionary conflict (Kick 1980, 1983).

Many of the interstate wars since World War II began as Third World Marxist insurgencies sponsored by the socialist semicore, led by the Soviet Union. These insurgencies have challenged the global economic supremacy of the capitalist core. As a consequence, revolutionary conflict in the periphery frequently has attracted intervention by core, semicore, semiperipheral, and peripheral states, who have provided military advisors, weapons, and troops. The political fragility of developing states invites these military interventions, especially where there is an economic and strategic advantage to be gained by the intervenors (Kick 1983). As regional allies of superpower intervenors are drawn into the fray, revolutionary conflicts spill over into neighboring countries and contribute to further regional militarization.

Dependency theorists argue that these dynamics have resulted in the pervasive militarization of the Third World, a militarization that hinders national development (Eide 1976). Third World countries are dependent on their superpower patrons for military aid, which increases the loyalty of the armed forces to their source of supply and reduces the commitment of the military to nationalism and nationalistic development. Even those Third World countries that have developed their own armaments industries for domestic use or export may not lessen their military dependency upon external parties. Third World weapons industries often require the purchase of ever more sophisticated technology (often computerized) sold only by core and semicore suppliers. Thus the militarized state is tied to the capitalist core and is an agent of repression that holds down wages and enforces the property rights of foreign capital. Third World armies also absorb revenue and skilled manpower that might otherwise contribute to economic and social development. In these ways, militarization acts as a brake on development in the Third World (Eide 1976, 318; Senghaas 1977, 104).

MODERNIZATION THEORY

According to many modernization authors, development is an indigenous process facilitated by a nation's ties to the industrialized world. It is through its links to the modern industrialized societies that a developing country can repeat the successful strategies of the developed world (Rostow 1960). A major part of the modernization process is a shift from traditional to modern technologies and institutions that stimulate the attitudes and values needed for efficient industrial production (Moore and Feldman 1960; Inkeles and Smith 1974; Chase-Dunn 1975; Portes 1976; Chirot and Hall 1981).

From the modernization perspective, armies and the armaments technology of the Third World help inculcate the modernizing attitudes necessary for domestic development. The military instills achievement motivation, discipline, and a willingness to cultivate foreign investment, which is viewed as a prodevelopmental force (Millikan and Blackner 1961, 112–13; Halpern 1962, 278–89; Pye 1962, 73–89; Stockwell and Laidlaw 1981, 300–301; Weede 1983, 11–18). Military regimes also integrate societies that have been divided by generations of conflict. Insofar as the officer corps is recruited from throughout the social structure, military socialization may also establish a far-reaching national identity (Lefever 1970, 179; Stockwell and Laidlaw 1981, 300–301). Military regimes may finally provide the domestic and international security that leads to political stability and development. Through these mechanisms, militarization benefits development in Third World countries.

EMPIRICAL EVIDENCE

Neither modernization nor world-system/dependency studies adequately explain the relationship between militarization and development. Many empirical studies focus on single countries only, rely solely on descriptive information about defense expenditures, or use study designs that are inappropriate for generating causal inferences (Malek 1968; Stepan 1971; Kennedy 1974; Kaldor 1976; Sivard 1981; Nordlinger 1970, 1977; McKinlay and Cohan 1975). As a result, the reported findings have been mixed and inconclusive (Benoit 1973; Weede 1983; Ball 1983; Lim 1983; Faini, Annez, and Taylor 1984; Biswas and Ram 1986; Deger 1986).[4]

One reason the militarization-development controversy has not been resolved is that prior studies emphasize different components of development. For instance, although modernization authors (Benoit 1973) are centrally concerned with economic development, world-system/dependency authors also consider repression and human rights (Eide 1976). Moreover, militarization is a multidimensional phenomenon. Different aspects of militarization affect the various dimensions of development in different ways (Kick and Sharda 1986). Militarization-development relationships may, in addition, vary greatly, depending upon the developmental attributes of countries (for example, whether the country is "developed" or "developing").

To examine these possibilities in the ensuing analyses, two cross-national equations are estimated, one for per capita economic production and the other for domestic political rights. The regression analyses attempt to measure the net effects of independent variables such as investment rates, foreign power-dependency linkages, and several measures of militarization on two different indicators of development for the world as a whole and for the Third World only.

METHODOLOGY

Sample

A "whole world" sample of fifty-nine countries and a Third World sample of thirty-nine countries are used. Countries were deleted from the original population if data were missing on any dependent or independent variable. The use of the two samples permits a comparison of militarization-development relationships, which may be different in the Third World than elsewhere, and also makes possible the assessment of the effects of all the world-system positions (core, semicore, semiperiphery, periphery) on development. For example, the relative effects of core versus peripheral position cannot be assessed in the Third World models, which are composed of semiperipheral and peripheral nations only. The countries in the analyses are shown in the appendix to this chapter, table 3.3.

Dependent Variables

The two measures of development are per capita gross domestic product (GDPC) in 1982, taken from the United Nations (1985), and Gastil's index of basic political rights in 1979, taken from Taylor and Jodice (1983, 58–61). The political rights index includes political liberties and measures justice based on autonomy for groups and individuals.

Independent Variables

World-System Position. World-system position variables are based on Kick's (1987) world-system classification (presented in the Appendix, table 3.3). The classification provides an operational definition of the Third World and identifies dummy variable regressors representing world-system positions.

There is extensive discussion elsewhere on the world-system classification used here (Kick 1987) and on the utility of network approaches as a mechanism for operationalizing the structure of the modern world-system (Snyder and Kick 1979). Nevertheless, some specifics of the network results warrant attention. They bear on important controversies about the use of economic and noneconomic linkages in identifying world-system structure and nations' positions within it.

The structure of the international system is operationally defined in the world-system position measure according to eight types of international interactions: export flows, bilateral economic aid and assistance treaties, bilateral transportation and communication treaties, bilateral sociocultural treaties, bilateral administrative and diplomatic treaties, political conflicts, armament transfers, and military conflicts.[5]

The inclusion of noneconomic, transnational linkages in the operationalization of world-system structure has become controversial. World-system and dependency writers frequently emphasize the centrality of transnational economic linkages in their treatment of the world system. Political, military, and sociocultural linkages are far less commonly emphasized. Yet these noneconomic linkages are mechanisms that are crucial to the operation of the world-system, even if they (necessarily) do not perfectly reflect the power-dependency links of the world-economy (Galtung 1971; Chirot 1977; Modelski 1978; Chase-Dunn 1980;

Zolberg 1981; Szymanski 1981; Ray 1983; Bergesen 1983). The distinction here between world-system and world-economy is international and important. The world-system embraces the multiple power-dependency links that tie nations together and form an international structure that intimately affects national processes and attributes (for example, development).

How are noneconomic links central to the operation of the world-system? Consider first that cooperative political ties between nations enable the flow of information concerning local political, economic, and strategic conditions. For powerful states, these ties provide a means for the global manipulation of conditions that may greatly affect their economic and political-military futures (for example, investment opportunities, strategic outposts, and direct interventions). Interstate political conflict may by the same logic sever the information flow and undermine the international (military, economic, political, and cultural) dominance of core and semiperipheral countries.

In a similar way, the transfer of conventional armaments permits arms sellers to exert power over recipients regardless of geographical remoteness. Arms transfers give "donors" the leverage that is invoked for later political, strategic, and economic concessions from the target country (Albrecht et al. 1974). Military conflict is also used to subvert or support the polity and economy in target countries. In many instances, it is a functional alternative to other economic and noneconomic control mechanisms when they fail (Galtung 1971), 100). Regional and global military dominance also determines international economic power through access to investments and markets.

Consider too that the international division of labor in transport and communications permits the global gathering of information by powerful countries about local political-military and economic conditions. These links ensure physical access to remote areas, access that is vital to the identification of cheap labor as well as marketing opportunities. They also provide global knowledge concerning strategic dynamics and foster intervention meant to affect the course of these events. There is also an important degree of global control associated with the production and dissemination of news on a worldwide basis (for example, Radio Free Europe).

Finally, sociocultural ties in the world-system enhance the availability of labor for foreign enterprises and are crucial in attracting intellectual talent (the "brain drain") to already-dominant international actors. They further technical ties such as scientific projects that, with technological advances, increase the technical and related economic, political, and military dependency of client countries on their external sponsors. Sociocultural links also are a powerful mechanism for the socialization of dependent populations (for example, student and research personnel exchanges). They help ensure ideological conformity between host and sender countries and secure the economic and political-military alignments between them.

Taken together, economic and noneconomic ties between nations appropriately reflect the structure of the world-system. They are mutually reinforcing dynamics that capture a global structure based on power-dependency links and not solely on economic links between countries.

The algorithm CONCOR was applied to these linkages between countries, resulting in a four-tiered partitioning of the world-system—core, semicore, semiperiphery, and periphery. Some implications of the four-tiered structuring of the world-system are discussed elsewhere (Kick 1987). For present purposes, dummy variables are constructed for each of the four tiers, and one tier is necessarily excluded as the comparison category in each of the models estimated.[6]

Militarization and Conflict. Five indicators of militarization and conflict are included as independent variables in the analysis. The average number of soldiers per capita, 1970 through 1975, is used to measure the "military participation ratio" (U.S. Arms Control and Disarmament Agency 1982; see Benoit 1973; Weede 1983). Dependency theorists argue that greater commitment of human capital to the military will be counterdevelopmental, while modernization theorists emphasize the prodevelopmental effects of military participation and the modernizing attitudes that accompany it. A dummy variable coded one for military regimes and zero otherwise (Sivard 1981) is included to judge whether military regimes are effective in instilling the unity and discipline that promote development or whether they are repressive and hinder development. The average annual ratio of weapons exported (U.S. Arms Control and Disarmament Agency 1982) divided by gross national product (GNP) 1970–1975 is included to ascertain whether the arms exports strategy adopted by Third World countries has positive or negative types of domestic economic or political spinoffs (Eide 1976). The frequency of civil war and the frequency of interstate war during 1967–1980 (from Small and Singer 1982) is included to address the possibility that conflict per se either assists development or hampers it (Kennedy 1974).

Other Independent Variables. In addition to world-system, militarization, and conflict variables, other causal agents are incorporated into the regression equations for the purposes of model specification. Neoclassical economic arguments maintain that higher domestic savings investment rates accelerate the domestic development growth process (Solow 1956; Swan 1956). To capture this dynamic, domestic capital formation is included as a regressor in our models. It is measured by gross domestic investment per capita in 1970 (Bornschier and Heintz 1979).

Finally, the economic development models incorporate a lagged dependent variable, measured in 1960 to account for the different initial stages of development for the countries present in our sample (United Nations 1979). No comparable measure of political rights is available for 1960. Secondary school enrollment in 1970 is included as a regressor (World Bank 1983), since many writers have argued that educational attainment and political rights are causally related (for a review, see Bollen 1983).

FINDINGS

Table 3.1 presents regression results for the Third World sample and the whole world sample. Descriptive statistics are presented in the Appendix, table 3.4.

Table 3.1
OLS Estimates for the Third World and Whole World

Third World — GDPC82 — Whole World

BETA	t	VARIABLE	t	BETA
.893	*	GDPC60	*	.340
		SCORE	*	-.086
		SPERIF	*	-.243
-.053		PERIF	*	-.200
.288		GDIC73	*	.580
.118		WEAPEXP	*	-.118
.168		MPR		-.014
.020		MILREGIM		.006
-.054		INTERWAR		.019
-.004		CIVWAR		-.008

| .851 | | R^2 | | .983 |

Third World — POLRIGHT — Whole World

BETA	t	VARIABLE	t	BETA
.272		SER60		.206
		SCORE		.051
		SPERIF		-.369
-.308	*	PERIF	*	-.497
.086		GDIC73		.034
-.180		WEAPEXP		.055
-.145		MPR		-.097
-.570	*	MILREGIM	*	-.387
.002		INTERWAR		-.047
.178		CIVWAR		.100

| .545 | | R^2 | | .784 |

GDPC82 Gross Domestic Product per capita in 1982
GDPC60 Gross Domestic Product per capita in 1960
SCORE Member of second tier (semicore) of world-system
SPERIF Member of third tier (semiperiphery) of world-system
PERIF Member of fourth tier (periphery) of world-system
GDIC73 Gross Domestic Investment per capita circa 1973
WEAPEXP Weapons Exports as a percentage of GNP, 1970–1975
MPR Military Participation Ratio, 1970–1975
MILREGIM Military Regime (1 = yes), 1967–1980
INTERWAR Fraction of years with interstate war, 1967–1980
CIVWAR Fraction of years with civil war, 1967–1980
* The t ratio for OLS was significant at the .05 alpha level.

Table 3.1 results are presented after the inspection of residual patterns and removal of a few outlier cases, and after possible problems related to nonhomogeneous variances ("heteroscedasticity") were considered. These latter problems were sufficiently negligible that OLS estimation procedures were judged appropriate. As in most cross-national studies of this type, multicollinearity, which rarely is addressed and treated in the literature, may pose some estimation difficulties. The possibility of its pernicious effects is examined in another set of estimations presented subsequently.

Table 3.1 results for the economic development variable show lagged dependent variable coefficients that are large (particularly for the Third World) and fully consistent with virtually all comparable studies (see, for example, Delacroix and Ragin 1981). Also consistent with prior treatments are (a) the significant negative effects, relative to the core, of world-system position; and (b) the positive effects of domestic capital formation for the whole world model. It is important to stress again that the world-system effects capture global power and dependency processes, not just economic links between countries. The absence of world-system effects in the Third World model suggests that domestic processes matter most in the relative development successes and failures of semiperipheral and peripheral countries.

The size of the capital formation coefficient, the coefficients for several of the militarization variables for the Third World model, and the pattern of bivariate associations (Appendix, tables 3.5 and 3.6) suggest that multicollinearity is a possibility in these estimations. Definitive judgments on the effects of these variables must be postponed, pending a more detailed examination presented in table 3.2. Note, however, that the effect of weapons exports on economic development is, for the whole world model, negative. Much more information is needed to determine in what types of countries weapons export programs deter economic development.

For the political rights models it is surprising that educational attainment does not impact political rights. This contradicts some major themes in political sociology (Bollen 1983); but again, the magnitude of this coefficient, the magnitude of others, and the intercorrelation among the regressors suggest that a reestimation is in order. In advance of that, it is noteworthy that peripheral position in the world system has a decidedly dampening effect on political rights, as does one key component of militarization, the presence of a military regime.

Table 3.2 presents results that permit us to better address possible technical problems related to multicollinearity. One result of high correlations among independent variables and their similar relations to the dependent variable is that the effected regression results may (through multicollinearity) mask real relationships. Specifically, multicollinearity inflates the standard error for regressors, which increases the risk of falsely rejecting a true relationship.

This condition is suggested by the bivariate associations reported in the Appendix, tables 3.5 and 3.6, and by the findings shown in table 3.2. Our table

Table 3.2
OLS Estimates Demonstrating Multicollinearity

GDPC82 for Third World

GDPC60	.626 *	.852 *	.883 *
GDIC73	.286		
MPR		.218 *	
WEAEXP			.184 *
R²	.791	.820	.807

POLRIGHT for Third World

MREGIM	-.507 *	-.531 *	-.541 *	-.460 *
PERIF	-.383 *	-.256	-.427 *	-.452 *
SER60		.237		
WEAEXP			-.237	
MPR				-.214
R²	.397	.436	.450	.436

POLRIGHT for Whole World

MREGIM	-.585 *	-.381 *	-.432 *
PERIF	-.385 *	-.647 *	-.187 *
SPERIF		-.555 *	
SER60			.494 *
R²	.540	.750	.716

GDPC82 Gross Domestic Product per capita in 1982
GDPC60 Gross Domestic Product per capita in 1960
SCORE Member of second tier (semicore) of world-system
SPERIF Member of third tier (semiperiphery) of world-system
PERIf Member of fourth tier (periphery) of world-system
GDIC73 Gross Domestic Investment per capita circa 1973
WEAPEXP Weapons Exports as a percentage of GNP, 1970–1975
MPR Military Participation Ratio, 1970–1975
MILREGIM Military Regime (1 = yes), 1967–1980
INTERWAR Fraction of years with interstate war, 1967–1980
CIVWAR Fraction of years with civil war, 1967–1980
* The t ratio for OLS was significant at the .05 alpha level.

3.2 estimations of the per capita gross domestic product and political rights models retain only the significant regressors from table 3.1 and other regressors that seem likely to be subject to masking effects. We drop regressors whose coefficients are near zero. Thus, since all of the nonsignificant regressors in the

GDPC82 model for the whole world have a trivial beta coefficient, the whole world GDPC82 model is not reestimated in table 3.2.

The new GDPC82 model for the Third World reports in three columns the effects of the lagged dependent variables and each of the regressors from table 3.1 that may be subject to masking effects. Note first that in column 1, domestic capital formation still has no statistically significant effect on per capita product. Capital formation and the lagged state of per capita product appear to share some of the same explanatory variance in the dependent variable. In contrast, the positive effects of the military participation ratio (column 2) and weapons exports now are visible. Their impacts on development were masked in the table 3.1 results, due to the pattern of intercorrelations among the related regressors when they were simultaneously incorporated into the economic development equation. These positive effects make plausible the contention of modernization authors that modernizing institutions and technologies related to the military generate developmental benefits in Third World countries.

Findings from the Third World political rights model are presented next. In column 1, the strong impact of military regime continues, as does the impact of peripheral position in the world-system (relative to semiperipheral position). Both effects are consonant with the themes of dependency theorists. However, despite some shifts in coefficient magnitudes, secondary education, weapons exports, and the military participation ratio still are unrelated to Third World political rights. This is in contradiction to conventional arguments about education and democracy and about the pro- or counterdevelopmental effects of militarization on development posited by world-system/dependency or modernization theorists.

Finally, for the whole world political rights model, both military regime and peripheral position continue to show their moderately strong and dampening influence on political rights. Semiperipheral position and secondary school enrollments (columns 2 and 3) now surface, too, as plausibly important determinants of political rights. Here the effect of education on democracy is consistent with prior theorization and evidence (see Bollen 1983). It appears justified to conclude that the patterns of correlation among the regressors, as shown in table 3.1, have hidden what are likely to be true substantive effects.

When taken together, the findings from tables 3.1 and 3.2 suggest that (a) world-system position variables exert a reasonably consistent and interpretable effect on economic development and on political rights for both the whole world and the Third World samples; (b) the effects of conflict and militarization are mixed—internal and international wars neither harm nor improve development across both samples; weapons exports dampen political rights to a marginal extent when the world as a whole is considered (but do not do so in the Third World); military participation has some positive effects on economic development among Third World countries; and military regimes are uniformly counterdevelopmental from the standpoint of basic political rights. While the consistency in relationships across the whole world and Third World samples is heartening from a technical standpoint, differences in relationships between the models suggest the possibility that standard model specifications (that is, theories) of economic and political development may not be universally applicable. For instance, conventional wisdom links education with democratic political systems (Bollen 1983), but this may not hold true among the countries that are on the periphery of the world-system.

There is a need in the world-system and dependency literature to treat seriously both economic and noneconomic links in the international system. The effects of the world-system position variable, an operationalization based on economic, military, political, and sociocultural networks, lends support both to world-system/dependency themes and to the contention that a multifaceted power-dependency approach to world-system structure is useful.

The key role of national militarization in affecting multiple forms of domestic development is a neglected area of research in the world-system and dependency literature. Results show that the different components of militarization affect development in different ways. For instance, the presence of military regimes greatly harms domestic political rights, while military participation and weapons exports appear to modestly encourage economic development in the Third World. These differences provide another reasonable explanation for the mixed results that characterize the literature on militarization-development linkages. They suggest as well that generalizations that identify uniformly negative or positive effects of militarization on development are overly simplistic. World-system and dependency writers have consciously distanced themselves from modernization arguments and ideologies, but what is needed is a world-system/dependency perspective that recognizes the more compelling themes from modernization approaches (see, for example, Chirot 1986).

It is interesting, too, that for the whole world sample, weapons exports hinder economic development. Coupled with the variable effects of education on political rights in the whole world versus the Third World samples, the variable effects of weapons exports suggest a need for more sample-specific theoretical propositions in quantitative world-system research. This conclusion may seem obvious, but there are numerous instances where reported results from essentially whole world samples may have been inappropriately generalized to the subsamples that comprise it.

In a related vein, the results show that careful attention to technical issues such as sample construction, outlier cases, heteroscedasticity, and multicollinearity is necessary in cross-national research of the type reported here. In the process of doing cross-national analyses of the world system, researchers often face radically different findings and conclusions that stem from comparatively minor differences in methodological strategies. These and related issues should be an increasingly important concern for quantitative world-system researchers.

NOTES

1. The authors are listed in alphabetical order. This research was partially supported by University of Utah Research Grants numbers 6–41554 and 2–15066. The authors wish

to acknowledge the contributions of Dr. Bam Dev Sharda in their earlier work examining the militarization and development relationship.

2. Such an approach also can plausibly lead to a structural approach that is centered on the many forms that power and dependency relationships take across diverse units of analysis (for example, the dyad, departments of sociology, nations, and the global system). It is noteworthy that this sociological approach to the world-system was well articulated by an international relations theorist, Johan Galtung (1971).

3. An exception to this is the work done by German dependency theorists (Kaldor, 1976).

4. For discussion, see, among others, Deger (1986).

5. Sources, coding decisions, and discussion of network densities for each network operator are detailed in Kick (1987).

6. For the whole world models, the excluded comparison category is the core. For the Third World models, the excluded category is the semiperiphery.

REFERENCES

Albright, Ulrich, Ernst Dieter, Peter Lock, and Herbert Wulf. 1974. "Armaments and Underdevelopment." *Bulletin of Peace Proposals* 5:173–84.

Ball, Nicole. 1983. "Defense and Development: A Critique of the Benoit Study." *Economic Development and Cultural Change* 31:507–24.

Benoit, Emile. 1973. *Defense and Economic Growth in Developing Countries*. Lexington, Mass.: Lexington Books.

Bergesen, Albert. 1983. "Modeling Long Waves of Crisis in the World System." In *Crises in the World System,* edited by Albert Bergesen. Beverly Hills: Sage Publications.

Biswas, Basudeb, and Rati Ram. "Military Expenditures and Economic Growth in Less Developed Countries: An Augmented Model and Further Evidence." *Economic Development and Cultural Change* 34:361–72.

Bollen, Kenneth. 1983. "World System Position, Dependency, and Democracy: The Cross-National Evidence." *American Sociological Review* 48:468–79.

Bornschier, Volker. 1981. "Dependent Industrialization in the World Economy: Some Comments and Results Concerning a Recent Debate." *Journal of Conflict Resolution* 25:371–400.

Bornschier, Volker, Christopher Chase-Dunn, and Richard Rubinson. 1978. "Cross-national Evidence of the Effects of Foreign Investment and Aid on Economic Growth and Inequality: A Survey of Findings and a Re-analysis." *American Journal of Sociology* 84:651–83.

Bornschier, Volker, and Peter Heintz, eds. 1979. *Compendium of Data for World-System Analysis: A Sourcebook of Data Based on the Study of MWCs*. Zurich: Sociological Institute of the University of Zurich.

Chase-Dunn, Christopher. 1975. "The Effects of International Economic Dependence on Development and Inequality: A Cross-national Study." *American Sociological Review* 40:720–38.

———. 1980. "Socialist States in the Capitalist World-Economy." *Social Problems* 27:505–25.

Chirot, Daniel. 1977. *Social Change in the Twentieth Century*. New York: Harcourt Brace Jovanovich.

———. 1986. *Social Change in the Modern Era*. New York: Harcourt Brace Jovanovich.

Chirot, Daniel, and Thomas B. Hall. 1981. "World-System Theory." *Annual Review of Sociology* 8:81–106.

Deger, Saadet. 1986. *Military Expenditure in Third World Countries.* London: Routledge and Kegan Paul.

Delacroix, Jacques, and Charles Ragin. 1981. "Structural Blockage: A Cross-national Study of Economic Dependency, State of Efficacy, and Underdevelopment." *American Journal of Sociology* 86:1311–47.

Eide, Asbjorn. 1976. "Arms Transfer and Third World Militarization." *Bulletin of Peace Proposals* 8:99–102.

Evans, Peter, and Michael Timberlake. 1980. "Dependence, Inequality, and the Growth of the Tertiary: A Comparative Analysis of Less-developed Countries." *American Sociological Review* 45:531–52.

Faini, Riccardo, Patricia Annez, and Lance Taylor. 1984. "Defense Spending, Economic Structure, and Growth: Evidence among Countries and over Time." *Economic Development and Cultural Change* 32:487–98.

Frank, Andre G. 1967. *Capitalism and Underdevelopment in Latin America.* New York: Monthly Review Press.

———. 1980. *Crisis in the World Economy.* New York: Holmes and Meier.

Galtung, Johan. 1971. "A Structural Theory of Imperialism." *Journal of Peace Research* 8:81–117.

Halpern, Manfred. 1962. "Middle Eastern Armies and the New Middle Class." In *The Role of the Military in Underdeveloped Countries,* edited by John J. Johnson, 277–315. Princeton: Princeton University Press.

Inkeles, Alex, and David Smith. 1974. *Becoming Modern: Individual Change in Six Developing Countries.* Cambridge: Harvard University Press.

Kaldor, Mary. 1976. "The Military in Development." *World Development* 4:459–82.

Kennedy, Gavin. 1974. *The Military in the Third World.* London: Duckworth.

Kick, Edward L. 1980. "World-System Properties and Mass Political Conflict within Nations: Theoretical Framework." *Journal of Political and Military Sociology* 8:175–90.

———. 1983. "World-System Properties and Military Intervention—Internal War Linkages." *Journal of Political and Military Sociology* 11:185–208.

———. 1987. "World-System Structure, National Development, and the Prospects for a Socialist World Order." In *America's Changing Role in the World System,* edited by Terry Boswell and Albert Bergesen, 127–55. New York: Praeger.

Kick, Edward L., and Bam Dev Sharda. 1986. "Third World Militarization and Development." *Journal of Developing Societies* 2:49–57.

Lefever, Ernest. 1970. *Spear and Sceptre: Army, Police, and Politics in Tropical Africa.* Washington, D.C.: Brookings Institution.

Lim, David. 1983. "Another Look at Growth and Defense in Less Developed Countries." *Economic Development and Cultural Change* 31:377–84.

McKinlay, R. D., and A. S. Cohan. 1975. "A Comparative Analysis of the Political and Economic Performance of Military and Civilian Regimes." *Comparative Politics* 8:1–30.

Malek, Anouar. 1968. *Egypt: Military Society, the Army Regime, the Left, and Social Change under Nasser.* New York: Vintage Books.

Millikan, Max, and Donald Blackmer, eds. 1961. *The Emerging Nations: Their Growth and United States Policy.* Boston: Little, Brown.

Modelski, George. 1978. "The Long Cycle of Global Politics and the Nation-State." *Comparative Studies in Society and History* 20:214–35.

Moore, Wilbert, and Arnold Feldman, eds. 1960. *Labor Commitment and Social Change in Developing Areas*. New York: Social Science Research Council.

Nordlinger, Eric. 1970. "Soldiers in Mufti: The Impact of Military Rule upon the Economic and Social Change in the Non-Western States." *American Political Science Review* 64:1131–48.

———. 1977. *Soldiers in Politics: Military Coups and Governments*. Englewood Cliffs, N.J.: Prentice-Hall.

Portes, Alejandro. 1976. "On the Sociology of National Development: Theories and Issues." *American Journal of Sociology* 82:55–85.

Pye, Lucien W. 1962. "Armies in the Process of Political Modernization." In *The Role of the Military in Underdeveloped Countries*, edited by John J. Johnson, 69–89. Princeton: Princeton University Press.

Ray, James. 1983. "The 'World-System' and the Global Political System: A Crucial Relationship?" In *Foreign Policy and the Modern World System*, edited by Pat McGowan and Charles Kegley, Jr. Beverly Hills: Sage Publications.

Rostow, W. W. 1960. *The Stages of Economic Growth*. Cambridge: Cambridge University Press.

Rubinson, Richard. 1976. "The World-Economy and the Distribution of Income within States: A Cross-national Study." *American Sociological Review* 41:638–59.

Senghaas, Dieter. 1977. "Militarism Dynamics in the Contemporary Context of Peripheral Capitalism." *Bulletin of Peace Proposals* 8:103–9.

Sivard, Ruth. 1981. *World Military and Social Expenditures*. Leesburg, Va.: World Priorities.

Small, M., and J. D. Singer. 1982. *Resort to Arms: International and Civil Wars, 1816–1980*. Beverly Hills: Sage Publications.

Snyder, David, and Edward L. Kick. 1979. "Structural Position in the World-System and Economic Growth, 1955–1970: A Multiple-Network Analysis of Transnational Interactions." *American Journal of Sociology* 84:1096–1126.

Solow, R. M. 1956. "A Contribution to the Theory of Economic Growth." *Quarterly Journal of Economics* 70:65–94.

Stephan, Alfred. 1971. *The Military in Politics: Changing Patterns in Brazil*. Princeton: Princeton University Press.

Stockholm International Peace Research Institute (SIPRI). 1987. *World Armaments and Disarmament. SIPRI Yearbook 1987*. Stockholm: SIPRI.

Stockwell, Edward, and Karen Laidlaw. 1981. *Third World Development*. Chicago: Nelson-Hall.

Stokes, Randall, and David Jaffee. 1982. "Another Look at the Export of Raw Materials and Economic Growth." *American Sociological Review* 47:402–7.

Swan, T. W. 1956. "Economic Growth and Capital Accumulation." *Economic Record* 32:334–61.

Szymanski, Albert. 1981. *The Logic of Imperialism*. New York: Praeger.

Taylor, Charles L., and David A. Jodice. 1983. *World Handbook of Political and Social Indicators*. New Haven: Yale University Press.

United Nations. 1979. *Yearbook of National Account Statistics Vol. 2. International Tables*. New York: United Nations.

———. 1985. *Statistical Yearbook, 1982*. New York: United Nations.

U.S. Arms Control and Disarmament Agency. 1982. *World Military Expenditures and Arms Trade, 1970–1979.* Washington, D.C.: USACDA.

Wallerstein, Immanuel. 1974. *The Modern World-System.* New York: Academic Press.

Weede, Erich. 1983. "Military Participation Ratios, Human Capital Formation, and Economic Growth: A Cross-national Analysis." *Journal of Political and Military Sociology* 11:11–19.

Wolf, Eric. 1969. *Peasant Wars of the Twentieth Century.* New York: Harper and Row.

World Bank. 1983. *World-Tables.* Vol. 2, *Social Data.* 3rd ed. Washington, D.C.: World Bank.

Zolberg, A. R. 1981. "Origins of the Modern World-System: A Missing Link." *World Politics* 33:253–81.

APPENDIX

Table 3.3

World-System Classification: Eleven Blocks for 130 Countries for a Multiple-Network Blockmodel, 1970–1975

CORE	1	Belgium[+], Canada[+], Denmark[+], France[+], West Germany[+], Italy[+], Japan[+], The Netherlands[+], Spain[+], Sweden[+], Switzerland, United Kingdom[+], United States[+]
SEMICORE	2	Bulgaria, China, Czechoslovakia, East Germany, Hungary, Poland, Romania, U.S.S.R., Yugoslavia
	3	Austria[+], Brazil[+], Finland[+], Greece[+], Lebanon, Norway, Portugal[+]
	4	Australia[+], Taiwan, Ireland[+], Israel[+], New Zealand
SEMI-PERIPHERY	5	Bahrain, India[+], Indonesia[+], Iran[+], Jordan, Kenya[+], Kuwait, Malaysia[+], Pakistan[+], Saudi Arabia, Singapore, Sri Lanka[+], Thailand[+], Turkey, United Arab Emirates
	6	Algeria[+], Cuba, Cyprus, Egypt[+], Ghana[+], Iraq, Liberia, Libya, Morocco[+], Nigeria, Syria, Tunisia, Zaire
	7	Argentina[+], South Korea[+], Malta, Mozambique, Philippines[+], South Africa, South Vietnam
	8	Bolivia, Chile[+], Columbia[+], Costa Rica, Dominican Republic[+], Ecuador[+], El Salvador[+], Guatemala, Guyana, Haiti, Honduras[+], Jamaica[+], Mexico[+], Nicaragua[+], Panama[+], Paraguay[+], Peru[+], Trinidad and Tobago, Uruguay[+], Venezuela[+]
PERIPHERY	9	Afghanistan, Angola, Bangladesh, Burma[+], Ethiopia[+], Malawi[+], Oman, Qatar, Sierra Leone, Somalia, Sudan[+], Tanzania[+], Uganda, North Yemen, South Yemen, Zambia[+]
	10	Benin, Burundi, Cameroon, Central African Republic, Chad, Congo, Gabon, Gambia, Guinea, Ivory Coast[+], Madagascar, Mali, Mauritania, Niger[+], Zimbabwe, Rwanda, Senegal[+], Tógo, Upper Volta
	11	Albania, Cambodia, North Korea, Laos, Nepal, North Vietnam

Note: Networks are defined with respect to linkages in exports, economic aid and assistance treaties, transportation and communication treaties, cultural treaties, diplomatic treaties, political conflicts, arms transfers, and military conflicts.

+ Countries included in the OLS regressions.

Table 3.4
Descriptive Statistics for Independent and Dependent Variables

Descriptive Statistics	Whole World		Third World	
	Mean	Std dev	Mean	Std dev
gross domestic product per capita, 1982 (current U.S. dollars)	3596	3949	1204	1049
Gastil's political rights index, 1979	4.305	2.087	3.179	1.587
soldiers per capita, 1970-1975	6.519	6.977	4.203	3.359
military regime=1, 1980	.322	.471	.462	.505
semicore=1, 1970	.136	.345		
semiperiphery=1, 1970	.508	.504		
periphery=1, 1970	.153	.363	.231	.427
frequency of civil war,1967-80	.047	.130	.071	.155
frequency of interstate war, 1967-80	.059	.143	.059	.140
weapons exported/GNP, 1970-75 (current U.S. dollars)	.000	.001	.000	.000
investment per capita, 1970 (current U.S. dollars)	244.3	288.7	69.38	65.85
gross domestic product per capita, 1960 (current U.S. dollars)	515.3	588.9	216.0	183.0
Secondary enrollment rate, 1960 (percent)	25.79	22.83	13.06	10.83

Table 3.5
Correlation Coefficients for the Whole World (N = 59)

	gdpc82	gdpc60	polright	soldiers	military	civil	interstate	score	speriph	periph	invest	weapexp	ser
gdpc82	1.000												
gdpc60	.924	1.000											
polright	.745	.684	1.000										
soldiers	.280	.247	.284	1.000									
military	-.418	-.418	-.628	-.155	1.000								
civil	-.279	-.279	-.236	-.198	.351	1.000							
interstate	.080	.177	-.033	.255	.150	.098	1.000						
score	.264	.170	.348	.502	-.167	-.145	.084	1.000					
speriph	-.557	-.458	-.396	-.254	.315	.116	.087	-.403	1.000				
periphery	-.348	-.306	-.450	-.263	.111	.185	-.130	-.168	-.432	1.000			
invest	.981	.897	.752	.311	-.437	-.276	.068	.294	-.577	-.321	1.000		
weapexp	.681	.799	.502	.402	-.294	-.154	.276	.035	-.418	-.188	.676	1.000	
ser	.899	.821	.728	.342	-.353	-.268	.177	.271	-.431	-.435	.899	.624	1.000

44

Table 3.6
Correlation Coefficients for the Third World (N = 39)

	gdpc82	gdpc60	polright	soldiers	military	civil	interstate	periph	invest	weapexp	ser
gdpc82	1.000										
gdpc60	.879	1.000									
polright	.203	.365	1.000								
soldiers	.325	.126	-.171	1.000							
military	-.036	-.054	-.500	.266	1.000						
civil	-.264	-.235	-.061	-.201	.289	1.000					
interstate	-.100	-.189	-.116	.454	.246	.130	1.000				
periphery	-.435	-.369	-.373	-.325	-.019	.114	-.170	1.000			
invest	.840	.885	.346	.123	-.115	-.287	-.161	-.353	1.000		
weapexp	.166	-.021	-.084	.434	-.137	-.009	.166	-.184	-.040	1.000	
ser	.535	.562	.315	.386	.112	-.168	.207	-.536	.542	.108	1.000

4

CORE WARS OF THE FUTURE

Christopher Chase-Dunn and Kenneth O'Reilly

Competition within the capitalist world-economy has periodically led to wars among the most powerful states of the system. If this pattern continues, many observers believe that human society, and perhaps three billion years of the evolution of life on earth as well, will come to an end. Therefore, it is important to assess the probability of future wars among core states.

Bergesen (1985) and Goldfrank (1987) have argued that the cyclical dynamics of the world-system have produced wars among core states in the past, and that these dynamics are likely to continue to do so in the future. But Arrighi (1982) concludes that future core wars are unlikely because of recent developments in the world-system. Given this disagreement among world-system scholars, we will review recent research on the relationship between world-system cycles and warfare and consider the combined effects of factors that both increase and decrease the probability of future core wars.

William H. McNeill (1982) has argued persuasively that the increasing efficiency of military technology, the rapid rate of technological innovation, and the geometric rise in the destructiveness of warfare over the last several centuries are the result of the interaction between a competitive market system and an interstate system composed of sovereign and competing states. By offering incentives for technological change and spurring economic growth, the market system provides resources for technological innovation that states can use to make war. The market system and institutions of international capitalism also reproduce the interstate system in which warfare is a legitimate form of conflict resolution.

In McNeill's analysis of military technology and military organization, the competition among sovereign states for scarce resources is a constant, but the availability of resources to engage in warfare and to fund arms races is an upward trend sustained by the growth of industrial production in the context of the world market. The increasing availability of resources for war and the application of scientific research and development and national education systems to military technology lead to escalation of rounds of competition for superior arms capabilities among core states. The development of new communications and transportation technologies increases the speed at which information about changes in military technology diffuses among competing states, further driving the trend toward more expensive and more destructive weapons.

THE K-WAVE AND WAR CYCLES

McNeill's description adequately captures the general trends we can observe over the past centuries, but it does not examine cyclical processes and the way in which they interact with the overall trends. There is a large corpus of studies of the timing, intensity, and causation of warfare among the great powers (reviewed in Levy 1983). There is also an extensive literature that examines business cycles in which prices and production growth rates vary cyclically over time. Recently attention has again been focused on the Kondratieff wave (K-wave), a business cycle with an approximately fifty-year period (actually it varies from forty to sixty years). The K-wave is most clearly indicated over long periods of time by changes in prices. Van Duijn (1983) has unambiguously demonstrated that K-waves occur synchronously on an international scale in the nineteenth and twentieth centuries.

One aspect of the link between the interstate system and the world-economy is revealed in the connection between the K-wave and warfare, first posited by Kondratieff himself. An impressive research literature has blossomed in recent years investigating this linkage, and although considerable disagreement still exists about the causal connections involved, quite a bit is now known.

International relations scholars have been working for decades to code the timing, participants, territory, costs, and destructiveness of warfare in the interstate system. Levy (1983) presents a recent complete compilation of the data on warfare. Although visual inspection of the frequency of wars and other measures reveals an obvious sequence of periods of more and less war, Levy reports that warfare does not exhibit any strictly cyclical features. Goldstein (1988, 244), however, demonstrates that a statistical test (the autocorrelation function) applied to Levy's data on war severity (the number of battle deaths per year) produces clear evidence of a fifty-to-sixty-year cycle over the period from 1495 to 1975.

Goldstein (1988) and Thompson and Zuk (1982) examine the relationship between this war cycle and the K-wave. Goldstein uses various price series and the dates given by four historical scholars (Fernand Braudel, Andre Gunder Frank, Nikolai Kondratieff, and Ernest Mandel) to produce a set of trough and peak dates for K-waves between 1494 and 1975. Goldstein argues that strict periodicity is an inappropriate standard for social cycles, and he analyzes sequences of phases with unequal periods in his measure of the K-wave. Goldstein shows a clear association between the K-wave and the severity (battle deaths per year) of war among core powers, and he finds that severe wars are much more likely to occur during the upswing phase of the K-wave. Thompson (forthcoming), who doubts the soundness of Goldstein's periodization of the K-wave before 1790, nevertheless finds support for the relationship between war and K-wave upswings in his own analysis of the period between 1816 and 1914. Goldstein's conclusion that war severity peaks during the K-wave upswing is very dependent on the cutting points he has chosen between phases, but what is not in doubt is the finding that the K-wave and the war cycle are linked in some systematic way.

The K-wave is most easily measured by price series. Goldstein argues that there is a production-stagnation cycle that precedes the price cycle by ten to fifteen years. In Goldstein's model, the war cycle peaks between the peaks of the production cycle and the price cycle.[1] The data on long-run series that indicate real production and related indicators are scanty, so most empirical work has focused on the relationship between price series and war because price data are more available. Some of the relationships between prices and warfare are well known. Governments at war print money and buy things, causing inflation. Thompson and Zuk (1982) have studied the relationship between price changes and warfare, and they report that most K-wave upturns (measured by prices) begin before the outbreak of wars.

Ernest Mandel (1980) outlines a Marxist explanation of the K-wave that focuses on capital investments in major types of energy and whole constellations of production technology such as steam power, railroads, electrical power, the chemical industry, computer technology, and so on. Related to this is the matter of the turnover time of fixed capital investments in private and public infrastructure. The structure of cities and transportation systems as well as plant locations and large-scale production technologies (such as steel mills) have a longer depreciation time than smaller investments such as individual machines. Public and private capital cannot rip up these major infrastructural investments every time technology changes, and thus these kinds of investments contribute to the rise of new, more productive competitors in distant regions (other states) and to the K-wave.

Adelman (1965) and others have argued that the K-wave is not an economic wave at all, in the sense that war and other "random shocks" such as revolutions are alleged to cause the K-wave. But if wars are random, why does the war cycle have a fifty-to-sixty-year period? Arnold Toynbee hypothesized a generational cohort effect that lasts for two generations (see Goldstein 1988, chapter

5). Allegedly both statesmen and citizens who have recently experienced war are unlikely to support new military adventures. But after two generations this reticence wears off and allows other factors to again produce intense warfare among core states. Thompson and Zuk's (1982) finding that K-waves start up before the advent of intense war periods does not completely contradict the hypothesis that war causes the Kondratieff upturn, because it may be argued that arms races and preparation for war begin to intensify well before the outbreak of hostilities.

Goldstein's causal model of the connection between war and the K-wave posits a negative feedback loop. According to Goldstein, wars occur during K-wave upswings because, though states always desire to go to war, warfare is expensive, and so states do it when economic growth is providing them with more resources. Warfare, on the other hand, has a negative effect on economic growth because it increases nonproductive expenditure and destroys people and property.

Like Thompson, Goldstein does not consider the capitalist nature of the institutions and processes that link warfare and economic growth in the modern world-system. For Goldstein, modern states are simply war machines that go after one another when they have the resources, and since capitalist economic growth provides great resources, warfare is endemic. While there may be some truth in this, it is important to consider the ways that geomilitary competition in a capitalist world-economy differs from such competition in a system in which the tributary mode of production is dominant. Capitalist states have different sorts of goals in warfare than do precapitalist states because surplus product is primarily appropriated through commodity production rather than tribute or taxation in a capitalist world-economy. Most importantly, the most powerful states in a capitalist interstate system do not pursue a policy of empire formation but rather act to reproduce the multicentric nature of the interstate system. Thus modern warfare is not merely an atavistic survival of precapitalist times that periodically grips a pacific capitalism, as Schumpeter (1955) argued. Rather, capitalism produces warfare and reproduces the political structure (the interstate system) that makes warfare legitimate (see Chase-Dunn 1989, chapters 8 and 9).

Goldstein's demonstration of the link between war cycles and the K-wave is extremely important evidence in support of the contention that geopolitics and the world economy are interdependent. His analysis of the warfare data results in the observation of four trends:

First, the incidence of great power war is declining—more and more "peace" years separate the great power wars. Second, and related, the great power wars are becoming shorter. Third, however, those wars are becoming more severe—annual fatalities during war increasing more than a hundred-fold over the five centuries. Fourth (and more tentatively), the war cycle may be gradually lengthening in each successive era, from about 40 years in the first era to about 60 years in the third. The presence of nuclear weapons has continued these trends in great power war from the past five centuries—

any great power wars in this era will likely be fewer, shorter and much more deadly. (1985, 432)

WARFARE AND THE HEGEMONIC SEQUENCE

Wallerstein (1984) has described a cycle of the rise and decline of hegemonic core powers (the Dutch, the British, and the United States). Modelski and Thompson (1988) have also discussed a "global power" cycle in which a single core state plays the role of world leader during some periods, followed by periods in which leadership is challenged by rising competitors and global war breaks out. Goldstein's analysis of the cycles is combined with a more historical consideration of the hegemonic sequence of the rise and fall of the Netherlands, Britain, and the United States. Although different scholars have different concepts of the nature of hegemony and leadership, they agree that the interstate system alternates between periods in which power is concentrated in a single hegemon and periods in which power is more equally spread among competing core states. These latter periods are agreed to be more conflict-filled and prone to warfare among core states.[2]

The process of empire formation was typical of most precapitalist world-systems, while in the modern world-system, neither hegemonic core powers nor their semiperipheral challengers have formed a single world state that could dominate the core region. This difference is largely due to the more fluid spread of technological development and the spatially uneven nature of capitalist economic development, which speeds up the emergence of new competing centers of core accumulation. The rapidity of the spread of new production techniques is facilitated by the capitalist institutions of commodified wealth, labor, and goods that allow market forces to strongly operate across large spaces. Though there has by no means been a completely free world market for labor and technology in the modern system, the frictions restraining the operation of international market forces are much weaker than in precapitalist world-systems.

The hegemonic sequence is cyclical only in a rough sense. The lengths of time involved in the rise and fall of hegemonies vary to some extent, and the periods between hegemonies are very unequal. Modelski and Thompson (1988) argue that the United Kingdom succeeded itself and thus served as a "world power" in two successive "power cycles." Goldstein observes that world wars do not always usher in new hegemonies, but that each new hegemony does follow a period of intense war among core states. Furthermore, the typical form of transition is for a rising challenger state (A) to initiate war against the declining hegemon (B). B makes an alliance with another rising state (C) to combat the military challenge by A. B and C win the war and C emerges as the new hegemon.

Regarding the relationship between the hegemonic sequence and the K-wave, Goldstein reports the following conclusions:

I find the connection between the causal dynamics of these two cycles—long waves and hegemony cycles—to be weak. They are not synchronized, and there is no exact number of long waves that "makes up" a hegemony cycle. Rather, I see the two cycles as playing out over time, each according to its own inner dynamic but each conditioned by, and interacting with, the other. (1988, 287)

Further along he concludes:

Each hegemony cycle contains several long waves, but not a fixed number. Each of the long waves *within* the hegemony cycle ends in a war peak that re-adjusts the international power structure without bringing in a new hegemony. (1988, 288; emphasis in the original)

CORE WAR AND UPSWINGS

Goldstein's empirical finding that the severity of war among great powers is greater during economic upswings contradicts what several other world-system scholars have argued. Andre Gunder Frank, for instance, writes, "Historically, the most acute political-economic struggles among rival economic centers and political states for hegemony typically take place during crisis 'B' phases" (1982, 120). B phases are the downturns of the K-wave during which economic growth stagnates. After describing the causes of stagnation during B phases, Wallerstein argues, "The result is a period of acute political struggle over the issue of distribution. . . . It can also take the form of acute interstate struggles, which can range from the use of mercantilist practices to the outbreak of local conflicts to the launching of those global civil wars we call world wars" (1982, 19).

Goldstein claims that there has been a misunderstanding of the relationship between economic cycles and war cycles because of the anomalous (for him) case of World War II, which occurred at the beginning rather than at the end of a long-wave upswing. This is the core war that most contemporary theorists think is typical. But Goldstein shows that its timing and severity with regard to the K-wave is the single exception to nearly 500 years of international conflict. He argues that the timing of World War II was influenced by the unresolved hegemonic situation that followed World War I, when the United States refused to take up the role of hegemon. His contention is supported by Wallerstein and others who see World Wars I and II as a single extended conflict.

Scholars agree that severe wars among core states are more likely to occur during periods of hegemonic decline when the old hegemon is vulnerable. Aspirants to hegemony or regionally expansionist states are more likely to seek to alter the international distribution of power by military means. Goldstein argues that these conflicts are most severe during A phases, and they typically occur near the end of A phases.[3]

The main reason why many world-system theorists have argued that warfare is more frequent during downturns is that they assume that competition for markets, raw materials, and profitable investment opportunities is greater during periods of economic stagnation, and this heightened competition encourages states to use military force to acquire these resources. But Goldstein argues that competition for scarce resources is also great during A phases and that states have more wealth with which to pursue expensive arms races and wars during A phases.[4]

CORE WARS OF THE FUTURE

Goldstein predicts that, barring major changes in the institutional structures of the world-system, another major war among core powers is likely to break out during the early part of the next century. He argues that the period of economic expansion following World War II was stabilized by the powerful golden age of U.S. hegemony, which was similar in some ways to the upswing phase from 1848 to 1872 during which the strong British hegemony coincided with a low level of core warfare. The B phase since 1970 is likely to turn again to an economic upswing in the 1990s, and Goldstein thinks that the pattern of core wars occurring late in upturn phases is most likely to recur, bringing on a period of maximum war likelihood in the second decade of the twenty-first century.

Goldstein's prediction of a new period of war among core states is based on his assumption that the institutional and structural conditions that produced the causal relationship between warfare and economic growth for the last 500 years has not undergone any fundamental change. The interstate system is intact; the boom-and-bust world market economy is continuing to expand and deepen; there is little prospect for the emergence of a new hegemonic power in the near or middle term; and U.S. power seems to be irreversibly in decline. Though Goldstein does not mention it, fossil-fuel shortages and the global shift in the balance between oxygen and carbon monoxide caused by pollution, which will heat up the earth and cause major inundations of coastal regions, may exacerbate international tensions and increase the probability of warfare.

But other world-system scholars have argued that a new period of core war is unlikely because of new conditions and unique features of the contemporary period (for example, Wallerstein 1982; Arrighi 1982). Their argument is based on the idea that nuclear weapons make war among core states impossible because it is unwinnable and therefore irrational. Recent progress in arms control negotiations may be the prelude to an era in which the still-sovereign core states ban nuclear weapons and therefore preclude both accidental and system-generated nuclear holocaust.

Giovanni Arrighi (1982) maintains that the current period of rapid globalization of production has led already to a situation in which interimperial conflict is less likely because the global capitalist class has become greatly interpenetrated and interdependent. Global sourcing by transnational corporations is seen as supporting evidence, as well as political expressions of this new level of international consortium such as the Trilateral Commission. A related argument points to the institutionalization of international organizations that can partially regulate political-military and economic competition and conflict. The International Monetary Fund has been credited with providing a mechanism that coordinates the

Figure 4.1
Factors Influencing the Probability of Future Core Wars

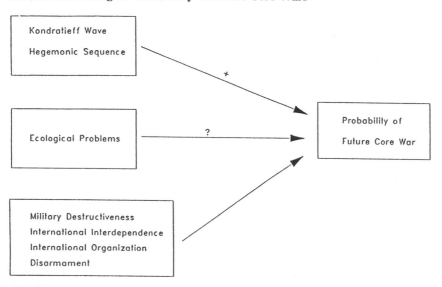

activities of international banks, thus averting an international financial collapse during the current debt crisis. The United Nations may not be able to guarantee collective security, but some observers claim that it has helped to avert core wars. Recent U.S. and Soviet progress in disarmament agreements has stimulated hope that the dismantling of weapons can reduce the likelihood of war.

To evaluate the probability of future core wars, we can analyze the relative strength of factors that are promoting or suppressing the likelihood of war. Simply listing these factors is the first step, which is done in figure 4.1.

Are all the major relevant factors included in figure 4.1? Perhaps other important processes should be included. Is causality represented too simply? There may be important interactions among the listed variables. Causal relations may not be linear, and the length of causal time lags may differ from variable to variable. Research on the past has shown that war severity is cyclical and that these cycles are known to be systematically related in time with some of the other causal variables. Different lags or cycle lengths can lead variables to reinforce or cancel each other's effects.

But if figure 4.1 roughly approximates the causes influencing the probability of future core wars, the next question concerns the relative weight of the factors listed. If the seven causes have equal weights, we can happily assume that the probability of future core wars is rather small, because the four negative factors will outweigh the three other factors. Examining such an assumption is difficult. At this point, all we can do is to consider whether or not the seven factors are getting stronger or weaker. We shall also discuss the unity of these factors and possible interactions. We will examine the seven factors in turn.

Kondratieff Wave

There is little reason to suggest that the effect of the K-wave on warfare has weakened. On the contrary, the expansion and deepening of the world market has probably brought global economic processes increasingly into phase with one another, as many observers of the effects of communications technology on stock markets and other institutions have concluded. Samir Amin (1974) noticed that shorter business cycles have been brought under greater control by the countercyclical policies of states, while the K-wave seems beyond the influence of state policy. It is possible that such countercyclical policies within states divert the shorter cycles of boom and bust toward the longer K-wave and increase the relevance of international competition for the long cycle. Such a trend, if it is indeed occurring, might produce stronger international economic competition and thus more strongly spur international military conflict. In any case, no one has argued that the amplitude of K-waves has decreased nor that their effect on other variables is weakening.

Hegemonic Sequence

Two trends may be observed in the hegemonic sequence. First, the hegemonic core state has gotten larger as a proportion of the world-system as a whole (however measured), and second, the rise and fall of hegemony has speeded up. It is hard to discuss trends when there are so few cases, however. Perhaps we can shed more light by looking at the particularities of the present period of U.S. decline.

Because the U.S. economy is itself such a large proportion of the world economy, its preponderance is prolonged in a number of ways. The size of the U.S. home market and the geographical and sociopolitical possibilities for capital flight within the borders of the United States (facilitated by a federal system that pits single states against one another) are other factors that slow down the decline of U.S. hegemony. Also, the relative size of the U.S.-based transnational firms is so great that it will take a long time for companies based in competing countries to catch up. Nevertheless, the fact that they have been catching up is well known, and there are indications that the United States has lagged behind competitors in the development of industrial policy and state-firm coordination (Bergesen and Sahoo, 1985).

If it is true, as Goldstein suggests, that the upturn of the K-wave after World War II did not produce core war because of the strength of the U.S. hegemony, it is also true that this factor will not operate as strongly in the future, but the exact rate of decline of this effect may be slowed sufficiently to have a retardant influence on core war in the next up phase of the K-wave. On the other hand, it is hard to imagine the emergence of a new core power to hegemony by peaceful means. Past hegemonic ascensions have always followed core wars. While there is a spate of upwardly mobile states, none of them by itself could constitute an economic and military power large enough to play the role of hegemon. More likely is a multipolar situation, or perhaps a bipolarity composed of two allied groups of countries. Wallerstein (1984) has suggested that the United States, China, and Japan might ally against Europe and the Soviet Union. Other combinations are certainly possible. Many political scientists argue that bipolarity based on multipower alliances is less stable than bipolarity based on two superpowers. Communications are more complicated, expectations are less stable, and defections are more likely. All this bodes ill for the period following the decline of U.S. hegemony insofar as the probability of core war is concerned.

Ecological Problems

Many observers claim that the scale of ecosystem disruption produced by contemporary and future industrial production will itself threaten the human species and the earthly biosphere in the near future. But what effects would global ecological problems have on the probability of core warfare?

The geometric increase in the use of fossil and nuclear fuels and synthetic chemicals has caused an upward trend in the scale and intensity of man-made disturbances to the processes of the biosphere, as well as global climatic changes. This trend may accelerate in the near future if greenhouse-effect forecasts are accurate. A substantial increase in the amount of solar ultraviolet radiation penetrating the atmosphere will raise the earth's temperature. This will melt polar ice caps, inundate coastal regions, change weather patterns, cause higher levels of cancer and blindness among animals (including humans), and alter food production patterns. The Soviet Union and Canada would likely increase their amount of arable land as the growing season lengthens. Other currently temperate areas will become tropical, and some areas will become arid.

The effect of natural disaster on political organization and action depends on a set of complex conditions and conjunctural circumstances. Disasters do not necessarily encourage cooperation, or, conversely, exacerbate tension and conflict, but the shift in relative economic power following global ecological disaster would destabilize the international political economy and might increase the probability of core war. People whose lives are disrupted may be more easily convinced to go to war, and nation-states that face critical resource shortages may be tempted to appropriate the resources of other nation-states by force.

There are, however, two reasons to think that global ecological disaster will not increase the probability of core war. The very fact that rational prevention of these potential disasters will require concerted international cooperation and regulation may generate support for international organizations and in that way help to reduce the probability of future wars. As Goldstein and others have argued, nations go to war when they have lots of resources. When they have few resources, they are less likely to undertake and sustain costly military conflicts. If this is true, then global ecological disaster may decrease the probability of war. At present, however, the global nature of environmental problems has not yet generated a high level of international cooperation. Rather, the structure of international conflict and inequality is reproduced in the discourse about international regimes concerned with environmental problems (Krasner, 1985). Individual core countries usually support only limited international regulation that is controlled by the wealthiest countries (the biggest financial contributors to international organizations). Third World countries, on the other hand, usually support a more comprehensive and worldwide approach that is controlled on a one-nation, one-vote basis, but their initiatives are rarely successful. While this pattern is not encouraging, things may change as ecological problems become more pressing.

Military Destructiveness

As McNeill (1982) has noted, the destructiveness of military technology has been increasing for thousands of years, but the rate has accelerated rapidly in the last few countries in the context of capitalist industrialization and increasing economic productivity. The mutually assured destruction of the contemporary nuclear balance of terror is simply the extension of a trend long in operation. The weapons available at the beginning of World War II were quite destructive, but this apparently did not make warfare unthinkable or irrational for many statesmen or their followers. Some now argue that because nuclear weapons are so much more destructive, warfare among the great powers is no longer possible. The absence of direct war among core powers since 1945 is said to prove the case.

While the destructiveness of nuclear weapons has reduced the probability of core wars, it has driven conflicts among core powers to be fought out in peripheral areas with conventional weapons, as recent wars have been. But the destructiveness effect may not be strong enough to eliminate the possibility of core wars. There is, for instance, some possibility that a nuclear exchange among core powers will occur by accident. As long as automated weapons are at the ready, machine or human error could set off a chain of events leading to unintentional war. One consequence of disarmament treaties would be to lessen the probability of accidental war.

But we are concerned with the systemic causes of war, not conjunctural accidents. We think that nonaccidental core wars are still possible despite mutually assured destruction. When other factors that lead to warfare among core states raise the level of international tension, wars beginning in peripheral areas using conventional weapons may easily escalate into nuclear exchanges when one side begins to lose. This could even happen after a series of treaties have dismantled nuclear arsenals, because nuclear weapons are likely to be rebuilt under the pressure of an ongoing conflict.

The pattern of nuclear proliferation among noncore states increases the likelihood of war. As the number of states that control nuclear bombs increases, stability of estimates of relative power, communications between adversaries, and the assumptions of rationality behind the behavior of states become more problematic. As Goldstein says, "Nuclear deterrence has not yet had to face the important test—how it performs in a period of economic upswing coupled with weakened hegemony" (1988, 367).

International Organization

International governmental agencies have become stronger ever since the Concert of Europe was formed after the Napoleonic Wars. The coordination of postal communications was one of the earliest functions undertaken by international organizations. Both formal organizations and the normative understandings embodied in international regimes can be understood as forms of governance at the global level. The trend toward greater international organization is somewhat cyclical, however. The greatest surges occur following core wars and during strong hegemonies, and the strength of these institutions declines as international competition and conflict reemerge. The level of institutionalization of global regulation by international organizations probably reached its highest peak during the 1950s and 1960s, and it has diminished somewhat since then, although probably not to a level lower than that of the previous period of multipolarity in the 1930s.

Most social scientists agree with Max Weber's view that state power ultimately rests on the "monopoly of legitimate violence." The effort to construct a world-level organizational basis for global "collective security," which is manifest in the United Nations, does not monopolize legitimate violence in the contemporary world-system. The sovereignty of nation-states, which is a fundamental part of the United Nations Charter, legitimates the use of military power and war by existing nation-states.

Talcott Parsons (1961, 1971) pointed to international law as the most important basis for his argument that an emerging global normative order is an important arbiter of interaction in the "modern system of societies." But Max Weber, the source of many of Parson's theoretical concepts, defines international law as outside his sociological definition of law, which turns on "the presence of a staff engaged in enforcement." Weber says, "As is well known, it has often been denied that international law could be called law, precisely because there is no legal authority above the state capable of enforcing it. In terms of the present terminology this would be correct, for we could not call 'law' a system the sanctions of which consisted wholly in expectations of disapproval and of the reprisals of injured parties, which is thus guaranteed entirely by convention and self-interest without the help of a specialized enforcement agency" ([1922] 1978, 35). The willingness of the most powerful players in world politics to simply disregard the decisions of the World Court demonstrates the continuing weakness of international structures for conflict resolution and collective security.

The same is true of the International Monetary Fund (IMF), which seeks to stabilize international monetary relations, a job that is easier when the hegemonic core state's currency functions as world money. Pfister and Suter (1987) have attributed the international financial order's ability to sustain a massive debt crisis without collapsing to the IMF's leadership in preventing a beggar-thy-neighbor approach to debt among the great private and state banks. This is an example of a growing international organization ameliorating (or postponing) economic disruption. Averting international financial collapse undoubtedly improves the chances for peace, but postponing it might make the collapse more disruptive when it comes and thus more likely to cause war.

Obviously it is incorrect to assume that all institution building in the realm of international organization will have similar effects on the propensity for war. Conflict resolution and collective security institutions are clearly the most relevant, although with these there may also be a problem of nonlinear effects. It may be that if the world-system were to approach the point of a central monopoly of legitimate violence (a real world-state), the danger of core war would actually increase rather than decrease. Wars are known to break out when a psychology of "we better get them before they get us" prevails. Such attitudes might well be rampant in a world-system in which world-state formation was imminent.

This does not appear to be an immediate danger, however. The conflict-resolving ability of the United Nations may have declined rather than increased in recent decades, along with the increasing multipolarity of the distribution of economic power. A call for a world constitutional convention to form a world federal state (actually an important movement after World War II) seems anachronistic now, despite the growing awareness that only a monopoly of legitimate violence can prevent nuclear holocaust. Nevertheless, if we compare the current and near-future situation with the 1930s, international regulation has probably reduced the propensity for warfare among core states to some extent.

International Interdependence

There are two basic questions that are important to the understanding of trends in global interdependence. The first looks at changes in the general level of specialization and exchange in the global economy and the extent to which the everyday lives of individuals have become materially dependent on the maintenance of a global system of production and exchange. This is akin to Durkheim's "organic solidarity." The second question focuses on relations among the different subgroups of the global bourgeoisie, the owners and controllers of the major means of production. This has gone under the label of the tendency toward "superimperialism," a cooperative approach among capitalists that eliminates the basis for wars among core states, versus "interimperial rivalry," the continuation of conflictive relations among national subgroups of world capital.

These two positions emerged before World War I in the debate among socialists about the coming of the "Great War."

Both the world economy as a whole and the interests of the world bourgeoisie have become more integrated and interdependent since World War I. Indeed, the growing internationalization of capital and increased spatial scale and density of commodity chains of production and consumption are long-term upward trends of the world-system that have been increasing since at least the seventeenth century (Hopkins and Wallerstein 1986).

Transnational corporations have long coordinated production and marketing across the boundaries between states and between the core and the periphery. The growth of their operations as a percentage of all economic activity, the extension of world sourcing and marketing, and the size of these firms have increased exponentially since World War II. But these firms are controlled by owners who are based in single nation-states. There are very few multinational corporations in the sense of firms that are controlled by approximately equal shares of capital from different states. Thus the formal control of property remains based in the interstate system, while the extent of operations has become increasingly transnational.

Those who argue that there has been a reorganization of the relationship among national fractions of the world bourgeoisie usually point to certain formal and informal international nongovernmental organizations that seek to coordinate the policies of core states and the interests of capitalists in different core states, such as the Trilateral Commission (Sklar 1980). The rather authoritarian political pronouncements that have been issued under the auspices of the Trilateral Commission (Wolfe 1980) contribute to conspiracy theories about a monolithic alliance of evil gnomes who are manipulating world events. Nevertheless, the actual performance of the Trilateral Commission leads to a different conclusion. Despite efforts to coordinate Japanese, U.S., and European international economic policies, there has been a definite drift toward economic nationalism and protectionism.

Giovanni Arrighi's (1982) argument, which stresses basic differences and discontinuities between the contemporary period of decline of the U.S. hegemony and earlier periods, claims that the international trade system has not moved toward protectionism during the recent K-wave downturn despite strong pressures to do so. This is a case where the cup is either half-full or half-empty. Despite the Reagan administration's ideological commitment to free trade, a number of "voluntary" quotas on imports have been legislated in recent years, and these euphemisms for protectionism are likely to become stronger in the Bush administration. Declining hegemonic core powers are always ambivalent about protectionism and display a zigzagging international economic policy. In this, the pattern being followed by the United States is not a departure. A strong and early turn toward a national industrial policy would be a departure if it were sustained, and this might slow the decline of the U.S. economy, but such a development would find little support from U.S.-based capitalists whose interests have become spread widely over the international economy.

Paradoxically, it is the capitalists of the declining hegemon who are most interdependent, and this undermines the use of political resources to make the U.S. economy more competitive in the world market. This, in turn, facilitates the further decline of the United States and decreases its ability to finance the costs of its military. Eventually, competing core powers will have to finance their own military protection, a development that will increase the likelihood of future core wars. Japan, for example, is extremely dependent on U.S. military power, lacking any autonomous capability to protect its vulnerable access to raw materials and markets. Rebuilding a Japanese military force would help to solve U.S. financial problems, but might lead to a less stable international military situation. A similar logic applies to Western Europe, particularly West Germany.

The increasing level of international interdependence is not likely to prevent war among core states. Transnational corporations remain very dependent on the power of individual core states to provide them with a profitable business climate. Although the Trilateral Commission seeks unsuccessfully to encourage coordinated international economic policies, no significant group of capitalists supports the formation of a world-state or even the further strengthening of the United Nations.

Disarmament

The recent treaties between the United States and the Soviet Union are heartening developments. For the first time, the superpowers have agreed to dismantle important weapons, and the prospects for further agreements of this kind are good. The major consequence of arms reduction is to lower the probability of accidental war, which is by no means an insignificant development.

A more comprehensive disarmament would probably reduce the likelihood of system-produced wars because the costs of rearmament for war would become greater. But destroying nuclear weapons while keeping conventional weapons does not eliminate the possibility of nuclear holocaust, because a serious and sustained war among core powers could easily escalate into a nuclear exchange when one side begins to lose. Rebuilding nuclear weapons would be likely in a desperate situation. It is the structure of the interstate system itself, together with these unbelievably destructive weapons, that threatens our future.

After reviewing the factors that might increase or decrease the chance of core wars, we can only estimate its likelihood. Nevertheless, it is our best guess that the developments that lower the probability of core war are not great enough to offset those factors that will increase the chance of war in the coming decades. The probability of serious war among core states over the next four decades may be as much as fifty-fifty.

The development of international mechanisms for conflict resolution among nation-states and the effective enforcement of the decisions of such agencies can help reduce the threat of future core wars. It may not be politic to refer to this as world-state formation, but that is what it is. Much important work has gone into "imaging" a peaceful world order (for example, Boulding 1988), but it is also important to identify the political forces that might support the strengthening of institutions of international conflict resolution and those who are likely to resist.

The weakest states most often support a strong level of international regulation that is democratically controlled. The most powerful states tend to oppose centralized regulation. Thus we can expect that many of the peripheral and semi-peripheral countries will support strengthening the institutions of international conflict resolution. The most powerful countries may well resist this, though some may support it. After all, everyone has an interest in the survival of our species. But the most powerful actors may be blind to the way in which the interstate system, with its multicentric structure of power among core states, is itself the problem. They will have to put their trust in a central confederation, which means that they will have to have a significant share of power in that confederation.

The United Nations, of course, embodies a balance between a democratic control structure (one nation, one vote in the General Assembly) and the allocation of power to the most powerful states (the Security Council and the veto power). Organizationally the United Nations must be able to eliminate the veto, which makes collective decision making very difficult, and increase the resources available to a multinational peacekeeping force. The most powerful states oppose changes of this sort, which means that the peace movements most crucial for moving toward increased international conflict resolution are those in the core states, particularly in the United States.

The peace movements' prospects are not entirely dismal. Peace movements in core states have been growing in recent years, and even during the Reagan administration a nationally funded peace research institute was established in Washington, D.C. The 1990s are likely to be a more fruitful era for progressive politics, if only as a response to the wave of conservatism we have experienced in the 1980s. The growing awareness of the cyclical processes of the world-system, the systemic nature of global war, and the need for structural change ought to spur the mobilization of a broad coalition in support of peace.

NOTES

1. Goldstein's analysis of ten production series confirms Imbert's (1959) hypothesis that production increases precede price increases. Goldstein finds that both ten- and fifteen-year time lags of the production series from the price peaks and troughs produce a largely regular sequence of down and up phases in six of the ten production series, and the differences in average growth rates between up and down phases are statistically significant (Goldstein 1988, table 10–4).

2. Efforts to operationalize contending definitions of hegemony and world power are described in Chase-Dunn (1989, chapter 9).

3. Goldstein distinguishes between two different economic cycles, a production cycle and a price cycle. In his idealized model, the peak of the production cycle is lagged behind the peak of the price cycle by about twelve years, and the war-cycle peak occurs just prior to the price-cycle peak. Some analysts have argued that stagflation, the combination of high unemployment and inflation (which seriously challenges most economic theories) is peculiar to the contemporary period and thus implies an important structural difference between the current era and earlier periods (for example, Arrighi 1982). Based on his conclusion that the price cycle is lagged behind the production cycle, Goldstein argues that stagflation is a recurrent phenomenon occurring in the period between the production and price downturns of the K-wave.

4. Some of the disagreements about the phase of the K-waves in which warfare is greatest may stem from Goldstein's finding that the two cycles are rather closely in phase with one another. Thus small differences in the dating of peaks and troughs could lead to different conclusions about the phase of the K-wave in which the war wave peaks. On the other hand, many of the earlier discussions seem to imply that the two cycles are completely out of phase with one another such that a peak in one corresponds with a trough in the other. Goldstein's research is strong against that possibility.

REFERENCES

Adelman, Irma. 1965. "Long Cycles—Fact or Fiction?" *American Economic Review* 55:444–63.

Amin, Samir. 1974. *Accumulation on a World Scale*. 2 vols. New York: Monthly Review Press.

Arrighi, Giovanni. 1982. "A Crisis of Hegemony." In Samir Amin et al. *Dynamics of Global Crisis*, 55–108. New York: Monthly Review Press.

Bergesen, Albert. 1985. "Cycles of War in the Reproduction of the World Economy." In *Rhythms in Politics and Economics*, edited by Paul M. Johnson and William R. Thompson, 313–31. New York: Praeger.

Bergesen, Albert, and Chintamani Sahoo. 1985. "Evidence of the Decline of American Hegemony in World Production." *Review* 8:595–611.

Boulding, Elise. 1988. "Imaging a World without Weapons." Workshop presented at the Conference on the Way to 2019: The Future of Vision, Gender and the American Dream, University of Akron, February 25.

Chase-Dunn, Christopher. 1989. *Global Formation: Structures of the World-Economy*. New York: Basil Blackwell.

Frank, Andre Gunder. 1982. "Crisis of Ideology and Ideology of Crisis." In Samir Amin et al., *Dynamics of Global Crisis*, 109–166. New York: Monthly Review Press.

Goldfrank, Walter L. 1987. "Socialism or Barbarism? The Long-run Fate of the Capitalist World-Economy." In *America's Changing Role in the World-System*, edited by Terry Boswell and Albert Bergesen, 85–92. New York: Praeger.

Goldstein, Joshua S. 1985. "Kondratieff Waves as War Cycles." *International Studies Quarterly* 29:411–44.

———. 1988. *Long Cycles: Prosperity and War in the Modern Age*. New Haven: Yale University Press.

Hopkins, Terence K., and Immanuel Wallerstein. 1986. "Commodity Chains in the World-Economy prior to 1800." *Review* 10:157–70.

Imbert, Gaston. 1959. *Des mouvements de Longue Durée Kondratieff*. Aix-en-Provence: La pensée universitaire.

Krasner, Stephen. 1985. *Structural Conflict: The Third World against Global Liberalism*. Berkeley: University of California Press.

———. 1987. "The United States and the Third World: Institutional Conflicts and Particular Agreements." In *America's Changing Role in the World-System*, edited by Terry Boswell and Albert Bergesen, 177–96. New York: Praeger.

Levy, Jack S. 1983. *War in the Modern Great Power System, 1495–1975*. Lexington: University Press of Kentucky.

McNeill, William H. 1982. *The Pursuit of Power: Technology, Armed Force, and Society since A.D. 1000*. Chicago: University of Chicago Press.

Mandel, Ernest. 1980. *Long Waves of Capitalist Development: The Marxist Interpretation*. London: Cambridge University Press.

Modelski, George, and William R. Thompson. 1988. *Seapower in Global Politics, 1494–1993*. Seattle: University of Washington Press.

Parsons, Talcott. 1961. "Order and Community in the International System." In *International Politics and Foreign Policy*, edited by James N. Rosenau, 120–29. New York: Free Press.

———. 1971. *The System of Modern Societies*. Englewood Cliffs, N.J.: Prentice-Hall.

Pfister, Ulrich, and Christian Suter. 1987. "International Financial Relations as Part of the World-System." *International Studies Quarterly* 31:239–72.

Schumpeter, Joseph. 1955. *Imperialism and Social Classes*. New York: Meridian Books.

Sklar, Holly, ed. 1980. *Trilateralism: The Trilateral Commission and Elite Planning for World Management*. Boston: South End Press.

Thompson, William R. 1989. *On Global War: Historical-Structural Approaches to World Politics*. Columbia, S.C.: University of South Carolina Press.

Thompson, William R., and L. G. Zuk. 1982. "War, Inflation, and the Kondratieff Long Wave." *Journal of Conflict Resolution* 26:621–44.

Van Duijn, J. J. 1983. *The Long Wave in Economic Life*. London: Allen and Unwin.

Wallerstein, Immanuel. 1980. *The Modern World-System*. Vol. 2. New York: Academic Press.

———. 1982. "Crisis as Transition." In Samir Amin et al., *Dynamics of Global Crisis*, 11–54. New York: Monthly Review Press.

———. 1984. *The Politics of the World-Economy: The States, the Movements, and the Civilizations*. Cambridge: Cambridge University Press.

Weber, Max. [1922] 1978. *Economy and Society*. Vol. 1, edited by Guenther Roth and Claus Wittich. Berkeley: University of California Press.

Wolfe, Alan. 1980. "Capitalism Shows Its Face: Giving Up on Democracy." In *Trilateralism: The Trilateral Commission and Elite Planning for World Management*, edited by Holly Sklar, 295–307. Boston: South End Press.

5

A Principal-Agent Analysis of the Initiation of War in Absolutist States

Edgar Kiser

The study of war is marked by fundamental disagreements about the impact of almost every significant causal factor. Does internal conflict make war more or less likely? Roughly equal numbers of studies have found a positive relationship, no relationship, and a negative relationship between internal conflict and inter-state war (see Stohl 1980). Are wars more frequent during periods of economic expansion or economic contraction? Goldstein (1985) suggests the former, whereas Wallerstein (1980, 25, 99, 158) and Hopkins and Wallerstein (1979, 494) argue for the latter. Are some types of states more prone to war than others? Several scholars have posited that war is more often initiated by autocratic states, but many others claim that democracies produce more frequent wars (see Waltz 1959, 120–21).[1]

The fact that the study of war has not progressed beyond centuries-old debates over basic issues suggests that there may be something wrong with our approach to this problem. Why has so little progress been made in studying such an important feature of social life? The first problem is one of method, broadly defined. Many have noted the atheoretical nature of most of the literature on war (Schelling 1960, 7–8); Boulding 1962, vii; Stohl 1980, 303; Bueno de Mesquita 1981, ix). Historicist and inductivist methodologies have guided most research. Some have argued that it is not possible to develop deductive theoretical arguments about the causes of war (Abel 1941; Aron 1960; Rapaport 1967). Because many scholars of war have rejected deductive theory, it has been difficult to accumulate a body of common knowledge. Until the study of war is guided by explicit, deductive theory, our understanding of it is not likely to be advanced (Kiser and Hechter 1988).

The second problem with the literature on war concerns theoretical assumptions. There are three common ways of explaining the decision to go to war, based on three different assumptions about which individual or group is making the decision. Most studies of war begin by assuming that the actors in international conflict are nation-states (for summaries of these arguments, see Wolfers 1959; Singer 1961; Allison 1971). War is explained in terms of the interests of nation-states and the structure of the system within which nation-states act. However, these studies do not explain whether this actor includes everyone in the nation, everyone in the government, or only the highest official in the state (Bueno de Mesquita 1980, 365–66). Most implicitly assume a unitary set of goals shared by all members of a nation (Allison 1971, 32–33). In order to avoid the problem presented by undefined corporate actors and the unreasonable assumption that all members of a society share the same interests, others begin by assuming that the actors in international conflict are the rulers of states (Boulding 1962, 152; Bueno de Mesquita 1981, 20). Since rulers are the sole decision makers, the frequency of war is seen as a function of their interests. A third group of scholars begins by assuming that the primary actors in the system are dominant classes, which presumably control states. For example, theories of imperialism (Hobson 1938; Lenin 1934) suggest that the main cause of war is the economic interests of capitalists (primarily in expanding markets).

Each of these theories has a similar problem. They all begin with assumptions about who controls political decision making. Some assume that a decision to go to war reflects the national or public interest, others assume that it reflects the ruler's interests, and still others assume that it reflects dominant class interests.[2] Each of these perspectives begins by assuming what must be demonstrated in any analysis of state policy: which individuals or groups have the power to shape state policies in their interests?

It is important to replace simplistic assumptions about who holds political power with a theory specifying the conditions under which different individuals or groups will be able to shape state policies. Two facts about decisions to go to war indicate the importance of such a theory of state policy formation. First, the interests of relevant actors (rulers, publics, dominant classes, and other groups) in war often differ. The group that controls or influences political decisions will affect the kind of decisions made. Second, the ability of rulers, publics, dominant classes, and other social groups to control state policies varies a great deal historically and cross-nationally. Most historians of war have noted these variations in interests and political power (Vagts 1937; Nef 1950; Ropp 1959; McNeill 1983) and have made numerous ad hoc arguments about their effects on the frequency of war in particular times and places.[3] Political scientists, sociologists, and economists are also aware of these two points and generally mention them in passing (for example, Bueno de Mesquita 1981, 20; Chase-Dunn 1981, 27; Lane 1979, 112; Tullock 1974, 88, 99). But they continue to make assumptions that preclude theoretical analysis of the ways in which variations in interests and political power affect the frequency of war.[4]

The initiation of war is a particular type of state policy. Therefore, an analysis of war must be built around a theory of state policy formation. The theory of state policy formation proposed here is based primarily on discussions of principal-agent relations in neoclassical economics. It will be used to analyze the initiation of war in absolutist Western Europe (roughly 1500–1789). This historical case is apposite for elaborating and illustrating a theory of the initiation of war because it is a period in which wars were relatively frequent and in which there were significant cross-national and temporal variations in the frequency of war.[5]

A PRINCIPAL-AGENT THEORY OF STATE POLICY FORMATION: THE DETERMINANTS OF AUTONOMY

A principal-agent relation is one defined by "a contract under which one or more persons (the principal(s)) engage another person (the agent) to perform some service on their behalf which involves delegating some decision-making authority to the agent" (Jensen and Meckling 1976, 308). Delegating authority, however, does not ensure that the agent will always act in the principal's interests. In fact, when the interests of the principal and the agent diverge (as they often do), I regard it as axiomatic that the agent will follow his or her own interests at the expense of the principal's interests. Thus the principal must find ways to control the agent's behavior. The degree to which principals are successful in setting up the rules of the game, monitoring the agent's actions, and instituting positive and negative sanctions to enforce compliance will determine the extent to which agents act in principals' interests (Berhold 1971; Hechter 1984, 1987).[6]

Two factors determine the extent of the agent's autonomy: (1) the relative resources of principals and agents (including their economic resources and capacity to engage in collective action) and (2) the ability of principals to control (that is, to set the rules, monitor, and sanction) the agent's behavior. These factors are interrelated in important ways. Resources are a necessary condition for principals to maintain most controls, and control is necessary to protect principals' resources. Autonomy is thus determined by the two factors jointly, not as discrete, separate variables.

Recent debates in political sociology have increasingly focused on the extent and determinants of state autonomy.[7] Some of the most important contributions to these debates have begun with the assumption that the state is potentially autonomous from social classes and have argued that the actual degree of state autonomy varies significantly.[8] Since the interests of the rulers of states and members of social classes often (though not always) diverge, these variations in autonomy result in variations in state policies. In other words, the reason that the study of autonomy is so important is that it provides the foundation of a theory of state policy formation. The main problem remaining in the current literature is the lack of a theory of state autonomy. Studies have replaced a flawed Marxist theory with only a negative statement (states are not tied to dominant classes, they are potentially autonomous) and a few particular historical analyses of states acting autonomously (Skocpol 1979, 1980; but Margaret Levi [1981, 1988] is a notable exception). Given that states are potentially autonomous, what is needed is a theory that specifies the determinants of variations in autonomy.

The general model of principal-agent relations outlined here provides the framework for such a theory, at least for autocratic states (Kiser 1987a, 1987b). Agency relations involve exactly the issues at stake in current debates about autonomy and state policies: agents are potentially autonomous, the interests of principals and agents often diverge, and there are constant conflicts over direct and indirect control of outcomes. Moreover, the principal-agent framework is sufficiently general to provide a theoretical analysis of both the traditionally Marxist topic of the relationship between rulers and classes and the traditionally Weberian issue of intrastate ruler-staff relations.

The autonomy of rulers of autocratic states (defined as the extent to which rulers are able to use state policies to realize their interests) is a function of the distribution of resources and control capacities at three different levels of principal-agent relations. The first is the relationship between dominant classes and the ruler. This can be described as the primary principal-agent relationship (where the dominant class is the principal and the ruler is its agent).[9] The second is the relationship between nondominant social groups as principals and the ruler as their agent. This is the secondary principal-agent relationship. Last is the relationship between the ruler and his staff. This is termed the internal principal-agent relationship. For the purpose of illustration, I will focus only on the primary principal-agent relationship and use examples exclusively from Western European absolutist states.

The dominant class gets the ruler to represent and enact its interest by relying on constitutional limits, monitoring devices, and sanctioning capabilities. Constitutional limits control both the legislative and fiscal powers of the state and the power of the ruler within the state apparatus. The detailed, written constitutions in England and Sweden (the Magna Carta and Magnus Eriksson's Land Law, respectively) clearly limited the legislative and fiscal powers of monarchs. Their existence made the task of monitoring monarchs much easier (the clarity of the limits made it easier to detect transgressions) and legitimated sanctions against those who violated constitutional dictates. The relative lack of constitutional limitations on royal power in France and Spain makes control of monarchs much more difficult. However, constitutional limits can only control the actions of rulers if they can be enforced, and for that, monitoring and sanctioning are required.

Monitoring involves gathering and disseminating information about the actions of the agent (Jensen and Meckling 1976). In the absolutist era, classes used remonstrances, judicial rulings, and tax auditing to monitor monarchs. For instance, *parlements* in France, controlled by the nobility, issued remonstrances whenever a law was passed by the king that violated their interests. The purpose of these remonstrances was to organize opposition to the law by informing members of the class that the king was acting against their interests. The judicial rulings of the English common-law courts performed a similar function.

Knowing what the agent is doing is only useful in conjunction with the capacity to sanction undesirable behavior (behavior that is not in the principal's interests) (Hechter, 1984, 1987). Two important sanctions were available to members of dominant classes in the absolutist era. When noble-controlled legislative assemblies had some fiscal powers, they could withhold tax revenues from monarchs who acted against their interests. For example, the English Parliament was often able to make the granting of taxes contingent on royal compliance with their demands. In France the dominant class, which had no national legislative assembly after 1614, could not employ this important sanction. In Sweden and Spain the legislatures lacked the right to initiate legislation and were thus unable to tie tax grants to the redress of grievances. The second sanction available was the failure to suppress peasant revolts against crown taxation. At times, nobles even instigated these revolts. The classic example of this is provided by the Fronde in France. In response to the centralization of power under Richelieu and the dramatic increase in taxes to fight the Thirty Years' War, the nobility led a fiscal revolt in which all classes participated.

Crown autonomy is a function not only of control capacities, but of the relative distribution of resources between principals and agents. Resources, including economic assets and the ability to act collectively, are important in three ways: (1) principals need resources to develop and maintain control mechanisms; (2) agents can use resources to subvert or avoid controls; and (3) resources are necessary to carry out state policies.

FROM AUTONOMY TO STATE POLICIES: INTERESTS AND POLICY PREFERENCES OF MONARCHS AND CLASSES

If there is some sort of unitary national interest (as many scholars of war seem to assume), then variations in autonomy will have no effect on state policies. However, there were wide variations in interests regarding war in the absolutist era. Therefore, state policies varied depending on which individuals or groups were able to shape state policy.

Two simplifying assumptions can be made at the outset: (1) all actors are rational egoists and (2) the most general interests of all actors are gaining and maintaining wealth and power.[10] These assumptions and knowledge of the structural constraints within which decisions are made can be used to derive the particular state policy preferences of various actors. An actor's decision to support or oppose a particular war will be based on his or her perception of the costs and benefits of the policy. Costs and benefits are determined by structural factors and will differ for groups and individuals in different structural positions. The constellation of forces supporting and opposing war policies will be a function of answers to two questions: (1) who pays the costs of war? and (2) who gets the benefits of war?

The cost-benefit calculations of each group not only depend on the direct costs and benefits of a particular action, but are always made relative to all other possible actions. Given limitations on time, money, and other resources, taking a particular course of action (such as spending money on war) precludes other actions (such as spending more money on roads and bridges). Opportunity costs can have an important impact on decisions about war.

RULERS' INTERESTS IN WAR

Rulers are more likely than any other individuals or groups to support war policies. The reason is that the benefits are many and varied, and most of the costs are paid by others. Rulers do not always support wars, however. A detailed analysis of the costs and benefits of war for rulers is necessary to answer more subtle questions concerning the structural conditions under which rulers will support wars, and the types of wars they will support.

There are two main types of benefits that rulers can gain from fighting wars: contingent benefits and intrinsic benefits. Contingent benefits require winning the war, whereas intrinsic benefits come simply from engaging in war. Contingent benefits can themselves be divided, depending on whether they provide immediate or long-term increases in a ruler's wealth. Immediate contingent benefits include taking land and exacting tribute from the losers in war. Long-term contingent benefits come from gaining control over state policies of the losers of wars. Policies are altered in ways that increase the wealth and/or power of the winning ruler, such as altering alliances or controlling trade routes (assuming that the ruler will gain from increased taxes on trade).

It is often rational for a ruler to fight a war he has little or even no chance of winning if the intrinsic benefits of fighting outweigh the contingent costs of losing. The main type of intrinsic benefit of war is the maintenance of social order by increasing internal solidarity (the perception of a unitary national interest). This is the primary argument made by those who suggest that internal conflict or unrest increases the frequency of war. Focusing on the (presumably shared) goal of defeating an external enemy aids the ruler if it decreases internal conflict, especially conflict against the state (Stohl 1980). At the very least, war provides jobs for the nobles who often lead revolts, removing them from the country (Kiernan 1980, 13). There are also some possible intrinsic economic benefits of war, including lowering unemployment (which may also reduce social unrest) and facilitating short-term growth (by increasing demand) in war-related industries.

The costs of war for rulers also can be divided into contingent and intrinsic costs. Contingent costs come only if the war is lost (and land or tribute is lost, or a change in policy is forced). Intrinsic costs are the resources expended in fighting the war and the opportunity costs of precluded policies. Intrinsic costs will be dependent on the size of the existing military apparatus—the smaller the existing military, the greater the intrinsic costs.

In order to assess the role of opportunity costs, it is useful to look at conditions affecting the ruler's choice between a policy of war and one of facilitating economic development. The most important difference between a war policy and an economic development policy is that the gains are distributed differently. What is important in determining whether or not a ruler will support a particular policy is not the total benefit (or cost) to the nation but the proportion of the benefit that goes to the ruler. Several predictions follow from this. First, it is generally the case that the proportion of the total benefit going to the ruler is greater for war than for economic development. Therefore, if the total benefits to the nation are the same for a war policy and an economic development policy, a ruler will support the war policy. For a ruler to support the economic development policy, its total social benefits must be larger than the total social benefits of the war policy by a factor great enough to make up for the difference in the proportion going directly to the ruler. Second, the extent to which a ruler supports a particular war will vary depending on the type of war, since the proportion of total benefits going to the ruler will vary. If the total benefits are the same, a ruler will give more support to a war to gain land that will go entirely to the crown than to a trade war, the benefits of which will go primarily to merchants.[11]

NOBLES' INTERESTS IN WAR

It is not possible to discuss the interests of nobles as a whole because of the high degree of stratification within the class. Although nobles are stratified quantitatively (between rich and poor nobles) and qualitatively (depending on their source of income), the focus here will be on the qualitative differences between three main noble groups: nobles employed as officers in the army, noble landlords, and nobles working as state officials.

Noble officers provided the only strong and consistent support for war among the nobility (Vagts 1937, 49–51). They stood to gain spoils while fighting, an opportunity to move up in the military ranks if they performed well (two intrinsic benefits), and a chance to share in the contingent benefits if the war was won. Since their benefits were primarily intrinsic, they tended to support all wars, regardless of the probability of victory (with the possible exception of cases in which victory was unlikely, gains were small, and death was likely). Moreover, their opportunity costs were minimal since they had little to do in periods of peace.

Noble landlords without positions in the state bureaucracy generally opposed war. For them, the costs were high and the benefits usually nonexistent. The amount nobles had to pay for war varied depending on the tax structure, but they always had to pay. When nobles had to pay taxes directly (as in England), their opposition to war was strongest. But even on the Continent, where nobles did not pay taxes directly, their ability to extract some of the limited surplus of peasant production in the form of rents was affected by state tax rates. When rulers raised tax rates to pay for wars, noble incomes often suffered. Thus noble landlords everywhere had to pay for wars, whether directly or indirectly. Since these costs were intrinsic, noble landlords tended to oppose all wars, regardless of the probability of victory. The form of the army also affected the costs of war for nobles. If a conscript army was used, laborers were removed from the fields, and rents could not only decline but go unpaid entirely.

Nobles in official positions in the state bureaucracy were generally indifferent or only slightly opposed to war, since neither the costs nor the benefits were particularly high. Since they were exempt from taxes, they paid no direct costs of war, and since they did not rely on income from rents, they paid no indirect costs. The only cost they were likely to pay was a debasement in the value of their office, caused by an increase in the sale of offices to meet the expenses of war. The only officials that had even a possibility of sharing in the gains of war were high-ranking officials who might (at the whim of their ruler) be given some of the spoils of a successful war. For this reason, some high-ranking officials supported war. But most noble officials had no hope of obtaining these benefits and thus were basically indifferent to war.

Noble landlords and officers were not fixed groups. There was a great deal of mobility between the two. Landlords could support a war policy if they wanted to become officers and realized that a larger army would increase their opportunities. Under what conditions did noble landlords want to become officers? This depended on the costs and benefits of each, including the salary and potential spoils for officers on the one hand and the rents available to landlords on the other. The rents available to landlords were primarily a function of the productivity of agriculture and the bargaining power of peasants. Therefore, the lower the agricultural productivity and the greater the bargaining power of the peasants, the more noble landlords tended to support war in order to change their status to noble officers. This relationship also had a dynamic aspect, since a war policy, by creating more officers, increased the size of the group supporting war and thus made additional wars more likely. Finally, the relationship between agricultural profits and support for war varied depending on the wealth of landlords, with the poorer landlords being more likely to support war than the richer noble landlords (since their opportunity costs of becoming officers were lower).[12]

MERCHANTS' INTERESTS IN WAR

Merchants' support for war depended on the scope of their markets. Domestic merchants always opposed wars. The costs to them were high because they were heavily taxed to pay for wars throughout the absolutist era. Furthermore, they did not benefit from anything that could be gained from war, such as land or control of trade routes.

For international merchants, the situation was more complex. As those who see state policies as a reflection of economic or class interests stress, international merchants often supported wars (for example, Wallerstein 1980, 78, 188, 191, 255–57). However, since they generally paid high taxes, the benefits of war had to be great to offset their costs. Only certain types of war provided such benefits. Wars for intrinsic benefits were not supported by merchants; their gains required that wars be won. They also did not support wars for land or tribute, since they did not share those benefits. The only wars they supported were those that promised to produce protection rents greater than the costs they paid in taxes (Lane 1979). Moreover, since their benefits were contingent on winning wars, they supported only wars in which the probability of victory was high.

Opportunity costs were also a significant determinant of merchants' support for wars. In general, the greater the ability of merchants to compete effectively in international markets, the less they tended to support trade wars to provide protection rents. War was an expensive and risky policy for merchants and was seen as unnecessary if their profits were already high. It follows from this that merchants in hegemonic countries (and to a lesser extent in all core countries) should have supported war least, and international merchants in semiperipheral and peripheral nations should have supported war most (controlling for the probability of winning).

FINANCE CAPITALISTS' INTERESTS IN WAR

Finance capitalists generally supported war in absolutist Western Europe (Vagts 1937, 40–45; Kiernan 1980, 268). Finance capitalists make money by making loans, and wars generally necessitate state borrowing. Wars increase the demand for their product, credit, and generally raise its price, interest rates. However, there was one condition under which finance capitalists would not support war: when rulers were not good credit risks. When debt burdens on rulers of absolutist states became too great, they often repudiated the debt. Therefore, if financiers believed that there was a danger of this, and if rulers wanted to borrow more money to fight a war that they were unlikely to win, finance capitalists might oppose the war. In general, finance capitalists' support for war was inversely related to the size of the existing debt.

PEASANTS' INTERESTS IN WAR

Peasants' interests with respect to war were simple and straightforward. They paid very high costs, both in taxes and with their lives if there was a conscript army; and they received no benefits, even if their nation won the war. The result of their cost-benefit analysis was consistent and strong opposition to war.

PREDICTIONS

How can theoretical arguments about political interests and power aid our understanding of the initiation of war in Western European absolutisms? The propositions listed here are intended to supplement and refine existing accounts of the causes of war, not to supplant them. Arguments about internal political processes can help resolve ongoing debates about the effects of internal conflict and economic cycles on war.

The first and simplest proposition follows from the argument that rulers will tend to support war more than any other relevant actors.

PROPOSITION 1: The higher the degree of autonomy of the ruler, the higher the frequency of war.

This proposition provides only the beginning of an explanation of the relationship between high autonomy and war. It is necessary to specify what kind of war will be most likely when autonomy is high. The first distinction concerns the types of benefits that highly autonomous rulers will seek.

PROPOSITION 2: The higher the autonomy of a ruler, the higher the proportion of all wars that will be fought for contingent benefits.

When autonomy is high, a ruler has very little need for the major intrinsic benefit of war: the creation of internal solidarity. Autonomous rulers can pursue policies in their interests without spending resources in this way. Only rulers with low autonomy will find it necessary to spend resources on creating solidarity.

This argument has important implications for the debate about the relationship between internal conflict and war. It suggests that there should be very little relationship between the two. When autonomy is high, the ruler has no interest in fighting wars for intrinsic benefits. When autonomy is low, the ruler does not have the power to fight wars (unless they are in the interest of some other group).

PROPOSITION 3: When the autonomy of a ruler is either high or low, there will be no relationship between internal conflict and the frequency of war.

There is only one special case in which rulers will have both the interest and the power to fight wars to increase solidarity in the face of internal revolts.

PROPOSITION 4: If and only if the autonomy of a ruler is moderate and declining, internal conflict will increase the frequency of war (fought for intrinsic benefits).

The inconsistent findings in the literature on internal conflict and war can be explained by the effects of variations in autonomy. No relationship should be the norm, with the one important exception noted here.

High autonomy has two other effects on what type of war is initiated. The first follows from the argument that highly autonomous rulers only fight wars for contingent benefits.

PROPOSITION 5: Highly autonomous rulers will only initiate wars in which their military capacity is greater than that of their opponent.

When autonomy is low, depending on which groups are powerful (see Proposition 14), wars with a low probability of victory may be initiated.

The final effect of high autonomy on the type of war initiated concerns the distribution of the benefits of victory. In general, the higher a ruler's autonomy, the greater the proportion of state policies that serve only the interests of the ruler. In the case of war, rulers will try to maximize their resources and maintain their power by fighting wars that benefit only them.

PROPOSITION 6: The higher the autonomy of a ruler, the greater the proportion of wars that provide benefits only for the ruler.

When autonomy is high, wars to gain land and to change policies of other states for primarily geopolitical reasons will be most common.

Internal political processes can also help explain some of the contradictory arguments and findings concerning the relationship between economic cycles and the frequency of war. Goldstein (1985, 415, 433) claims that economic expansion increases the frequency of war because it increases resources necessary to maintain and deploy large military apparatuses. Although it is certainly true that economic expansion increases a nation's resources, two additional questions must be answered before an increase in resources can be linked to war: who controls those resources? and is it in their interest to spend them on war?

The extent to which economic expansion increases the frequency of war depends on two related factors: the degree to which state revenue is tied to the performance of the economy and the autonomy of the ruler. Some types of revenue, such as direct and indirect taxes, will vary a great deal depending on the overall performance of the economy. If these are the primary forms of state revenue, economic cycles have a strong effect on the ability of rulers to go to war. However, if a ruler has ample revenue from sources not heavily dependent on economic performance, such as crown lands, sale of offices, or loans, economic cycles will have a much weaker effect on his ability to go to war.

PROPOSITION 7: The higher the proportion of a ruler's resources coming from sources not tied directly to economic performance, the weaker the relationship between economic cyles and war.

Existing sources of revenue are not immutable, but can be altered by highly autonomous rulers. Autonomous rulers will generally be able to raise tax rates and find alternative sources of revenue to finance wars even during periods of economic contraction.

PROPOSITION 8: The higher the autonomy of a ruler, the weaker the relationship between economic cycles and the frequency of war.

If war is viewed as a function of both the total resources available and the extent to which the ruler (with interests in war) controls those resources, two general propositions follow.

PROPOSITION 9: When an economy is expanding and the autonomy of a ruler is high, the frequency of war will be highest.

PROPOSITION 10: When an economy is contracting and the autonomy of a ruler is low, the frequency of war will be lowest.

So far, only the consequences of high autonomy have been examined, with low autonomy being defined only negatively (that is, the ruler does not have power). But an agent's low autonomy is a function of control exercised by some principal. Low autonomy thus raises a question: what principal has greatest control over state policy formation? The answer in absolutist Western Europe was often some faction of the nobility, the economically dominant class. The following propositions are based on the assumption that nobles have some control over state policies concerning war, and draw out the consequences of noble political power for the frequency of war.

Control of state policies is always costly for principals; it requires that they spend various types of resources. Principals will only exercise control over rulers when the costs of control are less than the costs of rulers acting in their own interests (that is, the costs of policies that may be contrary to the interests of the nobles). If the costs of control for noble principals are constant,[13] the extent to which some faction of nobles will use resources on control to prevent monarchs from going to war will be a function of the costs of war to nobles.

War is a very expensive policy and always necessitates high taxes. Opposition to war is based primarily on an unwillingness to pay these costs. Since the distribution of costs depends on who pays taxes and how much they pay, opposition to war is a function of the tax structure. If it is assumed that only some groups in any society will have the power (resources and control capacities) to prevent war when it is not in their interests, then the frequency of war will to some extent be determined by the extent to which those groups are taxed.

This discussion and Proposition 1 imply the following:

PROPOSITION 11: The more regressive the tax structure of a country, the higher the frequency of war.

If rulers generally support war, and those with the power to prevent this policy have no incentive to do so, then a policy of frequent war will result. Since the nobility was the most powerful group in this period, a corollary of Proposition 11 will be

PROPOSITION 11.1: The lower the taxes on the nobility, the higher the frequency of war.

This explains two of the most significant facts about war in the absolutist era: why it was so frequent (because the nobility was not usually taxed), and why it was less frequent in England than elsewhere (because nobles were taxed there).

In order to simplify some of these arguments, the nobility has been discussed as a unitary group. There are important differences within the nobility, and the distribution of power of nobles in various subgroups has important consequences for the frequency of war. For example, since landlords are the group of nobles most opposed to war,

PROPOSITION 12: The greater the proportion and power of noble landlords, the lower the frequency of war.

This relationship will hold for all tax structures (since landlords who do not pay taxes directly are hurt by high taxation of peasants), but it should be much stronger when noble landlords are taxed directly. The strength of the relationship should also increase as the cost of war increases. However, if agricultural profits for landlords fall too low, some may support a war policy in order to change their status.

PROPOSITION 12.1: If agricultural productivity is very low and/or peasant bargaining power is very high, there will be no relationship between the power of landlords in the nobility and the frequency of war.

The other major group of nobles consists of those employed in some capacity by the state. Since they do not pay the costs of war either directly or indirectly, they have little reason to oppose it.

PROPOSITION 13: The greater the proportion and power of the nobility whose sole or primary source of income is service in the state, the higher the frequency of war.

One consequence of this is that in addition to being a way to finance wars in the short term, the sale of offices actually increases the frequency of war (and thus the need for more revenue) in the long term. This proposition can be stated in a more general form:

PROPOSITION 13.1: The greater the size of the state and the greater the degree of noble monopoly of official positions, the greater the frequency of war.

One implication of this proposition is that countries in which the dominant class was a "service nobility" (for example, Prussia or Russia) should have engaged in war even more frequently than Western European absolutisms. The proportion of the dominant class in the military also has significant effects on war (Schumpeter 1955).

PROPOSITION 14: The greater the proportion and power of nobles employed as army officers, the greater the frequency of war.

Since the benefits army officers get from war are primarily intrinsic, this relationship holds for all types of war and does not depend on the probability of victory.

Nobles were not the only group in the absolutist era with the resources and control capacities to have some influence over decisions about war. Merchants at times had a great deal of power, and several predictions can be made about the consequences of their power for the frequency of war.

PROPOSITION 15: The greater the power of merchants, the lower the frequency of wars for land and wars for intrinsic benefits.

An even more general argument can be made about domestic merchants.

PROPOSITION 16: The greater the power of domestic merchants, the lower the frequency of war.

Since international merchants can gain great benefits from trade wars, their impact on war depends less on the tax structure than that of the nobility (whose costs are more significant than their benefits). Since merchants were always taxed, and generally at high rates, the important variable is how much they could benefit from trade wars. The extent to which they could benefit depended on their ability to compete in international markets without war. This was largely a function of their position in the world economy (Wallerstein 1974, 1980).

PROPOSITION 17: For all hegemonic countries, the greater the power of merchants, the lower the frequency of war.

PROPOSITION 18: For all nonhegemonic countries, and to a greater extent for those outside the core of the world economy, the greater the power of international merchants, the greater the frequency of trade wars.

Two caveats should be noted: the higher the tax rates on merchants and the weaker the military of a country, the weaker this relationship will be.

The impact of finance capitalists on the frequency of war is dependent on the level of existing debt. Two general predictions can be made.

PROPOSITION 19: When the level of state debt is low, the greater the power of finance capitalists, the greater the frequency of war.

However, when debt levels increase, financiers must be concerned about protecting their investments. In this situation, they will be more cautious about the type of war they support.

PROPOSITION 20: When the level of state debt is high, the power of finance capitalists is positively related to the frequency of wars with a high probability of victory and inversely related to the frequency of wars with a low probability of victory.

These twenty propositions represent a provisional attempt to use a general principal-agent theory of state policy formation to make some testable predictions about the relationship between internal politics and the frequency of war. Many of them will certainly turn out to be wrong, but perhaps two important points have been demonstrated: that progress in the study of war can be made by using general, deductive theoretical models; and that these theoretical models cannot make assumptions about the outcomes of internal political processes, but must explain them.

NOTES

1. This list could easily be expanded. For example, does uncertainty make war more or less likely? Is a bipolar system more prone to war than a multipolar one?

2. One scholar of war makes no assumptions at all about who controls state power but simply defines the state so vaguely that it incorporates all possibilities: "It should be understood throughout this article that state is used as a shorthand expression. It does not refer to any organism but rather, depending upon the context in which the word is used, to those making decisions on behalf of the people, those influencing these decisions, or all the citizens" (Werner Levi 1960, 411).

3. Most of the arguments made by historians tend to stress cultural causes of war (Nef 1950, 117–33; McNeill 1983, 64). The theory developed here will focus instead on material factors.

4. I do not intend to make a general argument against simplifying assumptions. They are necessary to develop any theory, including the one presented here. I am arguing only that these particular assumptions preclude the analysis of one of the most important causes of war: internal politics.

5. The principal-agent theory may be applicable to democracies as well, although these raise many complicated issues that I have not as yet resolved. The scope of the theory is at this point still uncertain.

6. The microfoundations of the principal-agent model come from rational choice theory. The exact assumptions made will be discussed in the section on interests.

7. For general summaries of recent theoretical work on the state, see Jessop (1982), Carnoy (1984), and Skocpol (1985). Unfortunately, all are incomplete because they ignore public choice theory.

8. See Skocpol (1979, 1980), Block (1977, 1980), and Margaret Levi (1981, 1988).

9. It may seem counterintuitive to view the ruler as an agent and groups in civil society as principals (and not vice versa). An analysis of state formation reveals that rulers are always initially agents, regardless of how much power they may assume eventually (see Kiser 1987b).

10. It may be objected that these assumptions are not descriptively accurate, which is of course true. The point of these assumptions is not to describe reality, but to lay the foundation for some testable propositions. The theory should therefore be judged by the accuracy of its predictions, not the descriptive reality of its assumptions.

11. Another interesting consequence follows from this. If rulers support economic development policies only to the extent that they benefit directly, and if the amount of a ruler's direct benefit is a function of tax rates, then the higher the tax rate, the more rulers will support economic development. This has the rather counterintuitive implication that high tax rates may facilitate economic development.

12. This general argument has been made in many historical contexts (Vagts 1937, 49–51; Wallerstein 1974, 312; Kiernan 1980, 12–13).

13. Control costs are of course not constant. They vary depending on opportunity costs and the structure of the state. More complete formulations of the theory should include this as a variable.

REFERENCES

Abel, Theodore. 1941. "The Element of Decision in the Pattern of War." *American Sociological Review* 6:853–59.

Allison, Graham. 1971. *Essence of Decision.* Boston: Little, Brown.

Aron, Raymond. 1966. *Peace and War.* Garden City, N.Y.: Doubleday.

Berhold, Marvin. 1971. "A Theory of Linear Profit-sharing Incentives." *Quarterly Journal of Economics* 83:460–82.

Block, Fred. 1977. "The Ruling Class Does Not Rule: Notes on the Marxist Theory of the State." *Socialist Revolution*, no. 33:6–28.

———. 1980. "Beyond Relative Autonomy." In *The Socialist Register*, edited by Ralph Miliband and John Saville, 227–42. London: Merlin Press.

Boulding, Kenneth. 1962. *Conflict and Defense: A General Theory.* New York: Harper and Row.

Bueno de Mesquita, Bruce. 1980. "Theories of International Conflict: An Analysis and Appraisal." In *Handbook of Political Conflict*, edited by Ted Robert Gurr, 361–98. New York: Free Press.

Carnoy, Martin. 1984. *The State and Political Theory.* Princeton: Princeton University Press.

Chase-Dunn, Christopher. 1981. "Interstate System or Capitalist World-Economy: One Logic or Two?" *International Studies Quarterly* 25:19–42.

Goldstein, Joshua. 1985. "Kondratieff Waves as War Cycles." *International Studies Quarterly* 29:411–44.

Hechter, Michael. 1984. "When Actors Comply: Monitoring Costs and the Production of Social Order." *Acta Sociologica* 27:161–83.

———. 1987. *Principles of Group Solidarity.* Berkeley: University of California Press.

Hobson, John. 1938. *Imperialism: A Study.* London: Allen and Unwin.

Hopkins, Terence, and Immanuel Wallerstein. 1979. "Cyclical Rhythms and Secular Trends of the Capitalist World-Economy: Some Premises, Hypotheses, and Questions." *Review* 2:483–500.

Jensen, Michael C., and William Meckling. 1976. "Theory of the Firm: Managerial Behavior, Agency Costs, and Ownership Structure." *Journal of Financial Economics* 3:305–60.

Jessop, Bob. 1982. *The Capitalist State: Marxist Theories and Methods*. New York: New York University Press.

Kiernan, V. G. 1980. *State and Society in Europe, 1550–1650*. New York: St. Martin's Press.

Kiser, Edgar. 1987a. "The Formation of State Policy in Western European Absolutisms: A Comparison of England and France." *Politics and Society* 15:259–96.

———. 1987b. "Kings and Classes: Crown Autonomy, State Policies, and Economic Development in Western European Absolutisms." Ph.D. diss., University of Arizona.

Kiser, Edgar, and Michael Hechter. Forthcoming. "Beyond Inductivism and Historicism: Toward a Theory-driven Methodology for Comparative-Historical Sociology." *American Journal of Sociology*.

Lane, Frederic. 1979. *Profits from Power*. Albany: State University of New York Press.

Lenin, V. I. 1939. *Imperialism, The Highest Stage of Capitalism*. New York: International Publishers.

Levi, Margaret. 1981. "The Predatory Theory of Rule." *Politics and Society* 10:431–65.

Levi, Margaret. 1988. *Of Rule and Revenue*. Berkeley: University of California Press.

Levi, Werner. 1960. "On the Causes of War and the Conditions of Peace." *Journal of Conflict Resolution* 4:411–20.

McNeill, William. 1983. *The Pursuit of Power*. Oxford: Basil Blackwell.

Nef, John U. 1950. *War and Human Progress*. Cambridge: Harvard University Press.

Rapaport, A. 1976. "Mathematical Models in Theories of International Relations: Expectations, Caveats, and Opportunities." In *Mathematical Models in International Relations*, 10–36. New York: Praeger.

Ropp, Theodore. 1959. *War in the Modern World*. Durham: Duke University Press.

Schelling, Thomas. 1960. *The Strategy of Conflict*. Cambridge: Harvard University Press.

Schumpeter, Joseph. 1955. *Imperialism and Social Classes*. New York: Meridian Books.

Singer, David. 1961. "The Level of Analysis Problem in International Relations." In *The International System*, edited by Klaus Knorr and Sidney Verba, 77–92. Princeton: Princeton University Press.

Skocpol, Theda. 1979. *States and Social Revolutions*. Cambridge: Cambridge University Press.

———. 1980. "Political Responses to Capitalist Crisis: Neo-Marxist Theories of the State and the Case of the New Deal." *Politics and Society* 10:155–201.

———. 1985. "Bringing the State Back In: Strategies of Analysis in Current Research." In *Bringing the State Back In*, edited by Peter Evans, Deitrich Reuschmeyer, and Theda Skocpol. Cambridge: Cambridge University Press.

Stohl, Michael. 1980. "The Nexus of Civil and International Conflict." In *Handbook of Political Conflict*, edited by Ted Robert Gurr, 297–33. New York: Free Press.

Tullock, Gordon. 1974. *The Social Dilemma*. Blacksburg, Va.: University Publications.

Vagts, Alfred. 1937. *A History of Militarism*. New York: W. W. Norton.

Wallerstein, Immanuel. 1974. *The Modern World-System Vol. 1*. New York: Academic Press.

———. 1980. *The Modern World-System Vol. 2*. New York: Academic Press.

Waltz, Kenneth. 1959. *Man, the State, and War*. New York: Columbia University Press.

Wolfers, Arnold. 1959. "The Actors in International Politics." In *Theoretical Aspects of International Relations*, edited by William Fox, 83–106. Notre Dame: University of Notre Dame Press.

Zinnes, Dana. 1980. ''Why War? Evidence on the Outbreak of International Conflict.'' In *Handbook of Political Conflict*, edited by Ted Robert Gurr, 331–60. New York: Free Press.

6

World War, the Advent of Nuclear Weapons, and Global Expansion of the National Security State

Gregory McLauchlan

During the course of the last world war, the United States assumed its hegemonic place in the world-system.[1] The Soviet Union also emerged from the war a world power, but it did not possess the attributes—a strong economy, a multiocean navy, and atomic weapons—of a global superpower. The war obliterated the German and Japanese bids for geographic empire. It greatly accelerated the decomposition of the British Empire and ushered in the wave of nationalist and anti-imperialist revolution that continues to this day. World wars are transformative events.

But world wars are much more than this. Indeed, it is precisely the conception of world war (and war in general) as an event that obscures our understanding of the complex and world-transformative processes of world wars. Social theory, including world-system theory, has generally treated war in a subordinate fashion. War is generally viewed as an interregnum in the course of development of states (societies) and the world-system. War is seen as an expression or outcome of forces and contradictions within societies, between states, or in the world-system as a whole. War then settles these contradictions (often only temporarily) and permits things to return to a normal course of development, that is, a course determined by factors and forces constitutive of society or the world-system.

In such a view, war is not seen as having a potentially autonomous significance, either as historical process or theoretical object. Ultimately, war is reduced to what is nonwar. War is explained, rather than being a potential (if partial) explanation of the processes of development of states and societies. The intellectual roots of such a view of war, for both Marxist-inspired and non-Marxist social theory, are to be found in liberalism, in the separation (always only partial) of market from state, and in the separation of the relations of production from the overt modes of military domination characteristic of previous modes of production. No doubt the Hundred Years' Peace, which coincided with the great upsurge of nineteenth-century social theory, also contributed to this view of war, as wars between nations gave way to a period of profound social transformation, class struggles, and revolution within European society. For Marx, capitalism and socialism confronted one another within the same society, not across a divided world of blocs and partitioned states. While Lenin brought war into the center of his analysis of the dynamics of international capitalism, he nevertheless also saw war as a purely instrumental phenomenon and thus theoretically secondary.

During earlier epochs the liberal view of war was somewhat justified. Compared with the twentieth century, death and destruction were relatively limited. Economic, technological, and political factors restricted the capacity of states to wage war. The state and the potential to pursue war were embedded in economy and society, and war was largely a function of economic and social factors.

But the processes of war and its peacetime analog, security, have become dislocated from their previous embeddedness in the movement of economy and society. In the present century, world wars have raged over the entire earth. By harnessing the great advances in industrial production and then science and technology, states developed the capacity to project military power around the world. World war and its offspring—nuclear weapons and cold war—have given rise to national security states that devote a considerable part of the economy, scientific research, and development to the creation of new means of destruction. No longer is the state's capacity for war (and the political relations that flow from this) so embedded in and limited by the state of development of the productive forces of civil society. The national security state itself organizes and directs a considerable part of those productive forces, and in the nuclear age, unlike previous ages, the capacity to destroy exceeds the ability to rebuild.

This dislocation is evident in the recent decline of American economic hegemony, a decline that is not reflected in a concurrent eclipse of nuclear military power vis-à-vis other states. The separation is especially evident in the (nuclear) World War III that has been simultaneously prepared and deterred for the past forty years. World War III cannot be explained simply as an expression of long-term economic trends or macrohistorical processes of change in the world-system. The character of contemporary politics, the state and the interstate system, and technology will also be implicated as causal factors of World War III, and we must look for such causes before the event. Today the nuclear state, with its capacity for global nuclear war, has the potential not merely to alter the development of the world-system but to end it altogether.

There is not one world-system but at least two. One is the world economy and division of labor. A second world-system is that comprised of the nuclear weapon-producing states, which is dominated by the United States and the USSR. The political economy of nuclear missiles is as real and consequential as the political economy of commodities and exchange (for example, Thompson 1980). In the postwar period, every meeting between an American and a Soviet head of state has been structured by nuclear politics and conducted in a discourse of nuclear power relations. In this second world-system, the Soviet Union has the status of a superpower, which is based on its nuclear power, not its economic power. In the case of the United States, the significance of the relative dislocation of military and economic power was not evident for the first two decades or so of the postwar period, for American nuclear superiority coincided with American global economic and political hegemony.

The world-system of nuclear states has its own rules. The requirements of deterrence dictate that each side constantly develop new weapon systems that can destroy the other should deterrence fail. The zones of the world-economy and the boundaries of (provisionally) sovereign nation-states are overlaid with zones of nuclear containment—whole regions of the earth marked off by invisible, and sometimes deliberately vague, lines. The superpowers have declared or implied that threats to their interests within these boundaries would provoke a nuclear response.

Nuclear deterrence has been powerful not only as a doctrine or geopolitical strategy, but also as an ideology. In the postwar West, the bomb has "guaranteed the peace of the world." It has been a central axiom of the nuclear state that U.S. nuclear weapons have prevented large areas of the world from being absorbed into the Soviet bloc, and that nuclear deterrence has prevented another world war between the major powers. In short, nuclear weapons are the modern, postwar basis of world perpetuation.

Nuclear weapons have revolutionized time and space. The world had been shrinking for centuries, but the advent of nuclear weapons, coupled with long-range aircraft and then missiles, greatly accelerated the compression of time and space. The bomb was not only the first total military technology, it was also the first truly global military technology. The theme of Wendell Wilkie's 1943 bestseller *One World*, that "there are no remote places anymore" has acquired new meaning in the nuclear age.

The revolution in time is equally striking. In the nuclear age, states first measured security in hours, the time it would take bombers to reach their territory, time that has been reduced to minutes in the age of intercontinental ballistic missiles (ICBMs). This development has had several profound effects on the state and the world-system of nuclear states. First, it has led to a shift from a military strategy based on the concept of mobilization, which required only relatively small military forces in peacetime and the capacity to mobilize industry over a period of years if war came, to a military strategy of deterrence, which requires large nuclear forces in a constant state of readiness. This shift of course has had numerous implications for economy and society.

The eclipse of geography and time with the advent of nuclear weapons has been the decisive development in the shift from geopolitics to technopolitics. No longer is the control of geography the most significant measure of military power and state security. The development and deployment of science and technology is now the crucial mode of state-directed expansion. In the nuclear state system, it is not geography but technology that stands between survival and destruction. Thus in the nuclear state, a large proportion of the nominally peacetime economy is devoted to military research and development; weapons systems (Trident, B–1, MX) are the largest military *or* industrial projects undertaken.

Another consequence is that the state now has unprecedented power all the time. Previously, the capacity of the state to wage war was dependent on its ability to mobilize industry and people and thus required the political support of the population. Full mobilization took years. But nuclear weapons require the state to mobilize popular consent and military power in advance. A few state managers literally have their finger on the button. This is the most fundamental way in which the mode of destruction has become relatively autonomous from the secular, traditional political and economic dynamics of society and the world-system.

One of the major projects of the nuclear state and technopolitics has been the development of technologies to gain back a small but crucial increment of the time lost with the advent of nuclear weapons. Over-the-horizon radar, distant early warning networks, and satellites are all designed to expand space and lengthen time. The nuclear state developed the first global modes of surveillance.

Indeed, the nuclear state has been the leading sector of technological and economic expansion in the superpowers, opening up new frontiers and leading the transition to a postindustrial mode of production. The advent of nuclear weapons and the nuclear arms race was the major stimulus to the race into space—the "final frontier"—which was an attempt to expand a shrinking world. Similarly, nuclear submarines opened vast regions under the world's oceans to military exploration and occupation. Where previous modes of geopolitical expansion had been horizontal on the earth's surface, the nuclear state brought with it major new modes of vertical expansion. Because expansion into these realms required huge financial and technological resources, it was the state, not capital, that opened the new frontiers.

The effort to regain time lost with the advent of nuclear weapons and the ICBM, and to expand lost space, seems to be approaching a limit. The central problem of a star wars system is to develop a computerized command and control system capable of flawlessly executing billions of calculations and decisions in the first minutes of a detected nuclear attack. There is no time for meaningful human deliberation in such a situation. A star wars system would delegate the power to launch an attack on other states to machines. The tendency here is for the technology of the nuclear state to eclipse the political moment itself, to preprogram the politics of nuclear deterrence and nuclear war. Again, star wars increases the dislocation of the world-system of nuclear states from other modes of political and economic development.

The development of nuclear weapons is associated with new, state-led modes of expansion, in which the state makes claims on society and the world under the rubric of "national security." This results in new modes of geospatial expansion, where new frontiers are opened up above the atmosphere and beneath the seas. The state takes a central role in the innovation of science and technology as control of technology, not the control of geography, becomes the core dimension of national security. Time becomes an important vector of expansion. The state makes expansive ideological claims, arguing that the continual expansion of nuclear systems guarantees the peace of the world.

In what follows, I will elaborate on three points regarding national security expansion. First, the overall point is that the advent of nuclear weapons both was a major impetus to national security expansion and involved a shift to an emphasis on new modes of national security expansion. U.S. participation in World War II was a global enterprise. Only the United States was able to take a truly global perspective on both the war and the requirements of postwar world organization. However, America's wartime expansion—rooted in geopolitics, economic mobilization, and Wilsonian internationalism—had limits. These limits were reached at Yalta, where the United States, the Soviet Union, and Great Britain agreed jointly to administer postwar world security, and where the United States acknowledged both the need for Soviet collaboration in maintaining world order and Soviet predominance in Eastern Europe.

Second, not only did World War II make the development of nuclear weapons possible, but social processes of war and strategic factors explain why the United States alone developed nuclear weapons. The Manhattan Project and the technology of nuclear weapons were the decisive factors in the emergence of the science-intensive national security state, where a continuous and large-scale program of scientific and technological innovation was now central to national security.

Third, in the weeks before and during the Potsdam Conference, U.S. state managers sought to integrate the arrival of nuclear weapons into American plans for the postwar world. The dramatic shifts in U.S. actions and policy between Yalta and Potsdam, where the United States sought to overturn a number of the Yalta accords and generally took a hard-line attitude toward Soviet positions, can be attributed to the new sense of global power and confidence resulting from sole possession of the atomic bomb. Further, this shift can be seen as a move from a worldview based on geopolitics to one based on technopolitics, where the global capacities and power of nuclear weapons allowed American state managers to abandon their earlier need for Soviet cooperation and articulate a new, expansive conception of American global interests and objectives. The successful development of the bomb in the last months of the war seemed to be the realization of Roosevelt's earlier vision that nuclear weapons would make it possible to control the peace of the world.

A new conceptualization of the relationship between world war, the state, and the development of the world-system is needed. There are two key elements of such a reconceptualization. First, war can generate autonomous modes of state-led expansion that go beyond economic-based modes of expansion in both time and space. Second, world war can be more usefully conceptualized as a social process than as an event. In such a view, the causes, dynamics, and consequences of war are not reduced to other, more fundamental social processes.

YALTA AND THE LIMITS OF GEOPOLITICS

The limits of U.S. global expansion were revealed most clearly at Yalta, where U.S. state managers acknowledged that the Soviet Union would play a major role, and that Soviet-American cooperation would be necessary to maintain postwar European security, which meant preventing a resurgence of German aggression. The Allies agreed to mechanisms for joint postwar control and dismemberment of Germany and established a process for setting reparations, which was a major Soviet objective at Yalta. In the background of American thinking was Roosevelt's view that the United States would not be able to keep troops in Europe for more than two years after the war. The atomic bomb was not yet a reality. Shortly U.S. armies and industry would begin demobilizing, and the United States would have to rely on additional means of guaranteeing postwar peace. Thus gaining Soviet cooperation was essential to maintain security.

Similarly, a central U.S. objective had been to secure Soviet entry into the war against Japan. At Yalta, the Soviets agreed to enter the war within three months of the German surrender, in exchange for a return of territory lost by Russia to Japan in the 1905 war and restoration of Soviet privileges in Manchuria, for which the United States would acquire China's consent.

At Yalta, the United States recognized a fundamental Soviet security interest in Eastern Europe. The agreement on Poland, the subject of the most intense debate at the conference, was a Soviet-American compromise that included Allied recognition of a reorganized pro-Soviet Lublin government and future elections. At the same time, the Soviets agreed to join a U.S.-dominated United Nations organization.

Yalta represented an attempt to create a postwar world order that incorporated the Soviet Union and included the Soviets as a major actor. This approach to the negotiations at Yalta was based upon the dominant geographic, military, and political realities of the time. The possession or control of geography was the dominant measure of the power realities. The Soviet Union had achieved huge military success, and Soviet predominance in Eastern Europe was the de facto reality, as was Anglo-American dominance in the West and almost everywhere else. In short, Yalta was rooted in geopolitics.

But Yalta was the last major example of the negotiation of traditional great-power geopolitics. Five months later at Potsdam, where the Allies were supposed to finish laying the foundations for a stable postwar peace, U.S. state managers exhibited a new, hard-line attitude toward the Soviets and sought to reverse or alter a number of key provisions of the Yalta accords, including reparations and

Soviet entry into the war against Japan. The main reason for the sudden and dramatic shift was that the United States had successfully tested the atomic bomb. Now control of technology, not geography, was the dominant measure of world power, and the bomb seemed to give the United States alone the capacity to control the peace of the world. Even before the successful test of the bomb made possible this decisive shift in American diplomacy and worldview, the expansive implications of nuclear weapons were recognized by those responsible for the top-secret atomic bomb program.

NUCLEAR WEAPONS AND NATIONAL SECURITY EXPANSION

If war is a major impetus to new modes of state-led expansion, then the advent of nuclear weapons can be seen as an important product of national security expansion. Historically war has stimulated technological innovation (McNeil 1982; Giddens 1985; Milward 1977; Greenberg 1967). But why did only Britain and the United States determine that an atomic bomb was feasible, and then only the United States (with British assistance) successfully undertake development of a bomb?

Before the war, Germany had been in the forefront of nuclear physics, and German science and science-based industries were among the most advanced in the world. But German strategy for the war emphasized speed and surprise, and the Germans sought to exploit the technological superiority they possessed at the beginning of the war (Milward 1977). The blitzkrieg was designed to avoid the costly, prolonged war of attrition represented in the trench warfare of World War I. Germany did not prepare for a long war and did not fully mobilize its economy for war until after it had suffered major battlefield defeats.

The Germans sought to improve existing weapons. They did not emphasize the long-term development of new weapons but stressed the development of tactical weapons, such as tanks and tactical air forces, that could concentrate great force at one place with great speed. Unlike the British and Americans, the Germans did not develop a strategic bombing capability, which is based on the concept of a war of attrition involving the destruction of enemy cities and productive capacity. Indeed, the Germans offered the British a truce on the bombing of civilian population targets to avoid the bombing of German cities. The British rejected this truce because they believed that they could exploit their superiority in the air and deliver a major blow to the German economy and morale through bombing (Quester 1966; Blackett 1948). The most spectacular German technological successes during the war, the V–1 flying bomb and V–2 rocket bomb, were named *Vergeltungswaffen*, "revenge weapons," denoting their development in response to British attacks on German cities.

The limited German time frame and emphasis on incremental advances and tactical weapons placed restraints on German scientific efforts. But the Germans also failed to achieve a rationalized large-scale mobilization of science for the war. German science remained subordinated to military control, and scientific research was fragmented and uncoordinated (Bush 1949, 99; Baxter 1947, 8–9; Compton 1956, 221–25; Groves 1962, 244–45). Nazi attacks on science in the early 1930s—especially on so-called basic science, which was often referred to by Nazis as Jewish science—and the simultaneous persecution of Jews had a destructive effect on the status and capacities of German science (Compton 1946, 15; Greenberg 1967, 71, 81).

It is doubtful that the Manhattan Project could have been undertaken in the United States in the absence of conditions of world war (for example, Groves 1962, 413). Congress would have had to debate and approve the huge appropriations necessary for development of an offensive weapon of mass destruction. Undoubtedly this would have aroused serious opposition by the isolationist, neutralist, and antiwar political forces that were dominant in American politics before the war. In the absence of war and without the cloak of complete secrecy, approval of the Manhattan Project would have been difficult to obtain. While this conclusion is speculative, it highlights the historical and social circumstances that made possible the development of the atomic bomb.

Yet if world war made development of the bomb by the United States possible, it did not make it inevitable. War can stimulate major scientific and technological development, but the mobilization of science to develop new military technology does not in itself account for the development of the atomic bomb. As Milward (1977, 180) points out, there are also strong countertendencies; mobilization for war creates conditions of scarcity, and there is pressure to concentrate available resources on projects that will make a certain and rapid contribution to the war effort. In short, war often slows or blocks some kinds of scientific and technological development.

In the United States, military leaders were not optimistic about the possibility of developing military applications of atomic energy during the war and did not push for its development. The argument advanced by some (Freedman 1981), that the development of nuclear weapons represented an extension of the Anglo-American military emphasis on strategic bombing, is not persuasive. The factors that were behind the emphasis on strategic bombing, not strategic bombing itself, led to the development of nuclear weapons. Both the British and Americans sought to minimize their casualties. Because they were not subject to invasion, the fear of which can be used to mobilize the population, British and American state managers needed to maintain domestic support for the war effort. Minimal casualties were seen as one condition of such support. As Army Air Forces commander General Henry Arnold said: ''It is a fundamental principle of American democracy that personnel casualties are distasteful. We will continue to fight mechanical rather than manpower wars'' (Parrish 1979, 38).

As a result, Britain and the United States placed great emphasis on the role of science in the war effort. The longer Anglo-American time frame for mobilization, which was made possible by their geographic isolation, made it feasible for them to look to science, which involved a longer cycle of research and development than the mass production of existing technology. These factors, along with the political and organizational efforts of top scientists such as Vannevar Bush, head of the Office of Scientific Research and Development, and President James Conant of Harvard University, who successfully convinced Roosevelt that science could play a central role in U.S. military preparedness, produced an organizational structure of science in the United States that was far superior to German science.

The success of U.S. science depended on four factors. First, scientists were given autonomy to pursue development of new weapons. They were not subordinated to direct military control. Second, the science mobilization effort was centralized and coordinated. Third, scientific projects received the resources to conduct numerous and large-scale efforts. Finally, top scientists had direct access to the highest levels of political authority, including the president, and were able to bypass military bureaucracy. All these factors contributed in crucial ways to the bomb's development.

In short, the atomic bomb was a product of social and political forces set in motion by world war. Atomic fission was discovered by Otto Hahn and Fritz Strassmann in Germany on the eve of the war. But while the German state had the capacity in peacetime to build an atomic bomb, it did not have the proclivity, or possibly even the capacity, to do so in wartime. By contrast, the U.S. state did not have the political capacity in peacetime to develop nuclear weapons, but war created both the material conditions and incentives necessary for the development of nuclear weapons. Had the discovery been made three to five years earlier, as James Phinney Baxter points out, and had Germany mobilized its scientific resources, "working secretly, she might have crossed the bridge between pure and applied science, and developed weapons that would have ensured her world dominion" (1947, 423). Had atomic fission not been discovered until after the war, we might still be living in a world without nuclear weapons.

FROM GEOPOLITICS TO TECHNOPOLITICS AND THE SCIENCE-INTENSIVE NATIONAL SECURITY STATE

The scientists and top state managers who supervised the Manhattan Project realized that they were participating in a historical transition of far-reaching consequences. The advent of nuclear weapons meant that there would no longer be time to mobilize the nation's resources over a period of years to defeat an enemy. In an age of nuclear weapons and long-range aircraft, geography would no longer be the insulating barrier providing the time for industrial mobilization. In short, the immense destructive power of nuclear weapons eclipsed the previous security functions of time and geography. The technological superiority of weapons—nuclear weapons—at the outset of a war could be decisive.

The Manhattan Project and the advent of nuclear weapons marked the transition from geopolitics, where industrial mobilization and the control or military occupation of geography is the central measure of power, to technopolitics, where the development and deployment of science-intensive technology becomes the dominant measure of power and security. The implications of this shift were recognized by Manhattan Project scientists and top state managers well before the bomb was tested. While military planners and industry were preparing for demobilization of war production and reconversion, members of the Interim Committee, the top-level policy group of Manhattan Project scientists and state managers, were planning a greatly expanded effort in the area of atomic energy and nuclear weapons (for example, Sherwin 1977, 295–304). While the war of production and geopolitics was coming to an end, the war of technopolitics in the impending nuclear age was only beginning. In abolishing the previous roles of geography and time, the technology of nuclear weapons went far to abolish the previous distinction between war and peace.

The social base of technopolitics would be the emerging science-intensive national security state, modeled in part on the experience of the Manhattan Project, where the state would support and coordinate scientific research with potential military applications on a national scale, incorporating many of the nation's leading universities and science-based industries. While industrial mobilization was the doctrine of geopolitics and the capital-intensive war effort, the doctrine of the emerging science-intensive national security state was technological superiority.

The identification of technopolitics as the ascendent mode of postwar national security expansion was made explicit by two of those who were most closely associated with the advent of nuclear weapons. In his 1943 speech at Harvard University, Winston Churchill stated that ''the empires of the future are the empires of the mind'' (1944, 185). Bush preferred an American metaphor for expansion in the title of his 1945 report, *Science—The Endless Frontier*. While geographic expansion and geopolitics had been limited by the size of the earth itself and had been in decline since the early twentieth century—the German and Japanese bids for geographic expansion representing the last, and failed, efforts at geographic empire—the potential for technopolitics and science-based expansion was seen to be unlimited.

POTSDAM: THE GLOBAL CAPACITIES AND VISION OF THE NUCLEAR STATE

The advent of nuclear weapons and technopolitics required new internal modes of national security expansion, a fact that was evident in an expanding science-intensive state. At the same time, the successful secret test of an atomic bomb at the beginning of the Potsdam Conference had a profound, global impact on the American view of the postwar world.

The language used by state managers to describe the impending atomic age indicates the bomb's historic and global significance. As early as 1943, ''Stimson already believed that atomic energy had created a new order in international relations'' (Hewlett and Anderson 1962, 276). Lord Cherwell (Churchill's scientific advisor) held the view that "whoever possessed such a plant [for producing fissionable material] would be able to dictate terms to the rest of the world" (Gowing 1964, 97). Bush, Cherwell's American counterpart, also surmised in mid–1942 that atomic energy might be "capable of maintaining the peace of the world" (Hewlett and Anderson 1962, 267). Arguing against informing other allies of the Manhattan Project in the spring of 1945, Churchill said that "this matter is out of relation to anything else that exists in the world, and I could not think of participating in any disclosure." Churchill rejected early proposals for some form of international control of atomic energy: "I do not believe there is anyone in the world who can possibly have reached the position [that is, development of the bomb] now occupied by us and the United States" (Gowing 1964, 360). Roosevelt wanted to "hold S–1 [atomic bomb] technology closely" in the postwar period and "thus control the peace of the world" (Hewlett and Anderson 1962, 328). Stimson's initial briefing for Truman on the bomb ended with the proviso that if the bomb were used properly, the United States "would have the opportunity to bring the world into a pattern in which the peace of the world and our civilization can be saved" (Sherwin 1977, 291–92).

The bomb was not viewed only as a military weapon. Four years of top secret Anglo-American diplomacy were concerned overwhelmingly with postwar issues and the global implications of nuclear weapons. At the Potsdam Conference, the expansive visions associated with the advent of nuclear weapons were clearly revealed. The conference began on July 15; the first atomic bomb test was undertaken in New Mexico on July 16. Indeed, Truman had delayed the conference so that the Americans would know for certain if they possessed what Stimson called their "master card" of diplomacy. The impact of the bomb on American leaders at Potsdam was primarily psychological, a fact that did not lessen its subsequent material effects. Again, the language American and British leaders used to describe their reactions to the successful test is indicative; no other development at Potsdam favorable to the British or the Americans was described in the terms reserved for the atomic bomb. Stimson recorded his reaction upon receipt of the report of the successful atomic test: "It was an immensely powerful document . . . well written and with supporting documents of the highest importance." He immediately briefed Truman and Secretary of State James Byrnes, who "were immensely pleased. The President was tremendously pepped up by it" and said "it gave him an entirely new feeling of confidence" (Alperovitz 1985, 198; Messer 1982, 103–4).

Churchill describes Truman's behavior at a plenary session the following day: "When he got to the meeting after having read this report he was a changed man. He told the Russians just where they got on and off and generally bossed the whole meeting" (Alperovitz 1985, 199). Many British leaders had a similar reaction to the successful test. "From that moment," Churchill recalled, "our outlook on the future was transformed." The arrival of the bomb meant that "we were in the presence of a new factor in human affairs, and possessed of powers which were irresistible" (Alperovitz 1985, 201; Bernstein 1972, 33).

Churchill met with Truman at Potsdam and presented his views on the significance of the bomb. It was a "miracle of deliverance." An invasion of Japan was not necessary. Several shocks of the "almost supernatural" weapon would convince the Japanese to surrender, and the Russians would not be needed to defeat Japan. At the same time, the British and Americans would now be able to deal with European issues "on their merits" (Hewlett and Anderson 1962, 390–91).

Indeed, what had been a central objective of American wartime diplomacy—securing a Soviet commitment to join the war against Japan—no longer figured in U.S. plans. There is even strong evidence that the United States now worked to delay Soviet entry into the war in the Far East.[2] Simultaneously, the United States took a new hard line on Eastern European issues in an effort to reduce Soviet influence in the region. The United States also reversed its approach to the problem of postwar Germany, refusing to agree on a sum for reparations and, contrary to the Yalta agreement that Germany would be treated as a single economic unit, insisting that each side draw reparations from its occupation zone, which excluded the Soviets from compensation from the economically advanced Ruhr.

THE MEANING OF POTSDAM

Many historians have pointed to the major shift in American attitude and diplomacy between Yalta and Potsdam (for example, Yergin 1977; Messer 1982; Alperovitz 1985). The crucial question then becomes, what did the arrival of the atomic bomb have to do with this general and especially rapid shift in American perspective and actions?

Regarding the Far East, the answer is straightforward and there is little controversy. The bomb gave American leaders confidence that they could end the war quickly, without Soviet help, and thus block the expansion of Soviet influence in Asia.[3] The bomb would guarantee American hegemony in Japan and a predominant American influence in the region more generally.

The evidence regarding Europe is more indirect, though there are statements indicating the bomb's anticipated significance for developments there, including, for example, Secretary of State–designate Byrnes's view that "our possessing and demonstrating the bomb would make Russia more manageable in Europe" (Sherwin 1977, 202). Yet some historians, such as Robert Messer, have argued that American use of the bomb as "the gun behind the door," or a diplomatic "stick," at Potsdam and the Council of Foreign Ministers meetings that followed failed to achieve American diplomatic objectives in Eastern Europe and elsewhere because the U.S. nuclear threat was "credible to neither side" when it came to issues such as Eastern European elections. For Messer, "The points at issue between the United States and the Soviet Union at this time simply were not relevant to such use of the bomb" (1982, 89). While agreeing that possession of the bomb greatly increased U.S. "strategic power vis-a-vis the conventionally

armed Soviet Union,'' he downplays the significance of this by arguing that
"that power was an abstract, last-resort threat that did not really apply to the
problems then exacerbating American-Soviet relations'' (1982, 89).

The problem with Messer's interpretation, and others like it, is the tendency
to see the bomb solely as a weapon, a thing. This is essentially an instrumentalist
view of nuclear weapons. But if the bomb did not really apply to the myriad
issues between the United States and the Soviets, why did top state managers
think that it did? How do we account for the statements by top state managers
both before and upon learning of the successful atomic test?

A more convincing interpretation is that the bomb was indeed relevant to all
the problems surrounding American-Soviet relations. Alperovitz provides the
most compelling analysis of the overall significance of the arrival of the bomb:

In the last analysis . . . the atomic bomb influenced the fundamental problem Truman
faced to an even greater extent than it did his tactics; by revolutionizing the problem of
European security the new weapon rendered trivial the considerations which had dominated Roosevelt's approach until his death. (1985, 221)

The revival of German nationalist expansion was a major concern of Roosevelt
and his advisors. At Yalta, this problem was confronted in geopolitical terms.
Continued cooperation with the Soviet Union was one element that would be
essential in keeping Germany in check, especially after U.S. troops withdrew
from the Continent.

In "revolutionizing the problem of European security,'' the bomb gave the
problem of postwar Germany an entirely new character. As in the Far East, the
United States no longer required Soviet military assistance in ending or guarding
against a future military threat. Truman's statement to General de Gaulle following Potsdam, that "the German menace should not be exaggerated,'' because
"the United States possessed a new weapon, the atomic bomb, which would
defeat any aggressor,'' confirmed this new perception (Alperovitz 1985, 221).
As Stimson put it, America now controlled the "final arbiter of force.'' American
leaders now contemplated a revived German economy, which would both contribute to European recovery and become integrated with the West.

The significance of the bomb was not in what it enabled the United States to
do (the conception of the bomb implicit in the instrumentalist view), but in what
it freed the United States from having to do: making concessions to and com-
promises with the Soviets in order to maintain European security and obtain
Soviet participation in the Pacific war. The renewed hard line in Eastern Europe,
where the United States now pushed for major political changes, the assurance
that the Pacific war would result in an exclusively U.S. victory, and the hardening
of positions on the economic future of Germany are all products of the new
sense of power and confidence associated with the bomb. The bomb provided
a tremendous impetus to national security expansion in Europe and Asia. It made

it possible for U.S. state managers to conceptualize a more expansive and ex-clusive U.S. role in Europe and Asia.

This shift in perspective did not require any specific or overt geographic claims. As Truman put it to de Gaulle, because America was the only state with nuclear weapons, "The peace problem . . . was therefore largely economic" (Alperovitz 1985, 247). There was no need for American leaders to elaborate any specific links between the arrival of the bomb and each question of diplomacy or each regional dispute, because the bomb essentially had the same implications for all the issues at hand. U.S. leaders believed that once the power of the bomb were demonstrated, the Soviets would be more cautious in their actions and claims—everywhere. While the geopolitics of Yalta was regional, based on the assessment of the interests of the three major powers in each region (the Balkans, Eastern Europe, and the Far East) and the current military realities, the technopolitics of Potsdam was global.

The advent of nuclear weapons reveals some of the broader aspects of the reconceptualization of the relationship between war, the state, and the world-system. Not only was the advent of nuclear weapons a product of social processes set in motion by world war, but the development of the bomb involved a rev-olution in the mode of destruction itself, where the relations between state, society, and the world regarding the problems of war and security are funda-mentally transformed.

The development of the bomb made possible the extension of external, global modes of national security expansion set in motion by the war, modes that were compromised and cut short in the geopolitics of Yalta. The timing of the advent of nuclear weapons is significant. The Manhattan Project achieved its objective at one of the most momentous political junctures in history. The global capacity of the bomb, together with the global possibilities opened by war, led to an expansive U.S. vision of the postwar world. Where Yalta represented an Amer-ican-dominated world order that included the Soviet Union, Potsdam represented a postwar world in which Soviet influence and power were to be denied.

NOTES

1. This work is based in part on my doctoral dissertation, "Nuclear Weapons and the Formation of the National Security State" (sociology, University of California at Berke-ley, 1988). More extensive discussion of a number of the arguments here, as well as more detailed documentation, can be found in this larger work. I would like to thank the University of California Institute on Global Conflict and Cooperation for supporting the research upon which this is based. I also thank Robert Schaeffer for his editorial contri-butions.

2. See, for example, Alperovitz 1985, 230; Bernstein 1972, 44–45; Messer 1982, 105; and Hewlett and Anderson 1962, 391. Additionally, this is only one of many factors that challenge the traditional view that the atomic bombings of Japan were undertaken mainly for military objectives, that is, to end the war quickly and save lives. American leaders

realized that a Russian declaration of war would have been the greatest additional military blow Japan could have suffered at this time, but now did not push for such a declaration.

3. Thus, for example, Truman concluded in his memoirs, "Our dropping of the atomic bomb on Japan had forced Russia to reconsider her position in the Far East" (1955, 425).

REFERENCES

Alperovitz, Gar. 1985. *Atomic Diplomacy*, expanded and updated edition. New York: Penguin.

Baxter, James Phinney, III. 1947. *Scientists against Time*. Boston: Little, Brown.

Bernstein, Barton. 1970. "American Foreign Policy and the Origins of the Cold War." In *Politics and Policies of the Truman Administration*, edited by Barton Bernstein, 15–77. Chicago: Quadrangle Books.

Blackett, P.M.S. 1948. *Fear, War, and the Bomb*. New York: Whittlesey House.

Bush, Vannevar. 1945. *Science—The Endless Frontier*. Washington, D.C.: U.S. Government Printing Office.

———. 1949. *Modern Arms and Free Men*. New York: Simon and Schuster.

Churchill, Winston. 1944. *Onward to Victory*. London: Cassell and Company.

Clemens, Diane Shaver. 1970. *Yalta*. New York: Oxford University Press.

Compton, Arthur Holly. 1946. "The Atomic Crusade and Its Social Implications." *Annals of the American Academy of Political and Social Science*, 9–19.

———. 1956. *Atomic Quest*. New York: Oxford University Press.

Freedman, Lawrence. 1981. *The Evolution of Nuclear Strategy*. New York: St. Martin's Press.

Giddens, Anthony. 1985. *The Nation-State and Violence*. Berkeley: University of California Press.

Greenberg, Daniel S. 1967. *The Politics of Pure Science*. New York: Plume Books.

Groves, Leslie R. 1962. *Now It Can Be Told*. New York: Harper.

Gowing, Margaret. 1964. *Britain and Atomic Energy, 1939–1945*. London: Macmillan.

Hewlett, Richard G., and Oscar E. Anderson, Jr. 1962. *The New World, 1939–1946*. Vol. 1 of *A History of the United States Atomic Energy Commission*. University Park: Pennsylvania State University Press.

McNeill, William H. 1982. *The Pursuit of Power: Technology, Armed Force, and Society since A.D. 1000*. Chicago: University of Chicago Press.

Messer, Robert L. 1982. *The End of an Alliance*. Chapel Hill: University of North Carolina Press.

Milward, Alan S. 1977. *War, Economy, and Society, 1939–1945*. Berkeley: University of California Press.

Parrish, Noel Francis. 1979. *Behind the Sheltering Bomb*. New York: Arno Press.

Quester, George H. 1966. *Deterrence before Hiroshima: The Airpower Background of Modern Strategy*. New York: John Wiley.

Sherwin, Martin J. 1977. *A World Destroyed*. New York: Vintage.

Thompson, Edward. 1980. "Notes on Exterminism, the Last Stage of Civilization." *New Left Review*, no. 121: 3–31.

Truman, Harry S. 1955. *Memoirs Vol. 1: Year of Decisions*. Garden City: Doubleday.

Wilkie, Wendell. 1943. *One World*. New York: Simon and Schuster.

Yergin, Daniel. 1977. *Shattered Peace: The Origins of the Cold War and the National Security State*. Boston: Houghton Mifflin.

7

Devolution, Partition, and War in the Interstate System

Robert Schaeffer

Some states are more prone to war than others. Since World War II, various forms of war—irregular guerrilla war, conventional interstate war, and the threat of superpower nuclear—have visited one group of countries: the "divided states."[1]

The divided states are countries that were divided by great (Great Britain) and superpower states (the United States and the Soviet Union) after a world war in this century: Ireland after World War I and Korea, China, Vietnam, India, Palestine, Cyprus, and Germany after World War II. Most of the divided states have experienced irregular, guerrilla or terrorist wars on their soil. Independence movements in all of these states except the two Germanies have campaigned against civilian populations and armed forces using assassination, bombing attacks, and guerrilla warfare to achieve their ends.

Most of these states have also waged conventional wars against their neighbors. The Korean and Vietnam wars have been among the bloodiest in the postwar period. Some of these wars have been protracted—the war in Vietnam lasted some thirty years, from 1945 to 1975—and some have been relatively brief, the six-day Arab-Israeli War being the shortest. They tend to recur. India and Pakistan have gone to war three times since they were divided in 1947. Israel and its Arab neighbors have gone to war five times since Palestine was partitioned by the United Nations in 1947. Most of these countries exist in a state of war with their neighbors, even those that have not fought a war in many years: China and Taiwan, and Israel and its neighbors have been at war for some forty years, the two Koreas for thirty-eight, and Cyprus and North Kibris for fourteen. Only Germany has not been visited by conventional war, but it has huge, mostly foreign standing armies drawn up on either side of the border dividing East from West. All told, irregular and conventional war in the divided states has taken nearly thirteen million lives in the postwar period, one-third of them civilian, and has affected the lives of the more than two billion people who live in divided states (Sivard 1987, 29–31).

These countries have also been visited by the threat of nuclear war. It is not widely known, but the United States has threatened to use nuclear weapons some twenty times since it attacked Hiroshima and Nagasaki. On fourteen, or two-thirds, of these occasions, the United States threatened one of the divided states.[2] North Korea, China, North Vietnam, India, and East Germany have all been threatened, most of them several times. The Soviet Union has threatened to use its nuclear weapons on fewer occasions—three or four times—but Israel and China have most often been the target of its threats (Kaplan 1981; Blechman and Kaplan 1981; Betts 1987; Halperin 1987). Having been threatened by nuclear-armed superpowers, many of the divided states began to acquire nuclear weapons of their own. China, India, Pakistan, and Israel have all developed nuclear weapons. South Korea and Taiwan are thought to be capable of doing so.

After reviewing the martial resumes of the divided states, one can say that war, in various forms, is common to all. War in the divided states tends to be obdurate and irremediable. There is no end in sight to the conflicts that keep divided states in states of war.

Historians and journalists usually give one of two explanations for conflict in the divided states, although no one has attempted to explain their collective history. The first explanation, usually applied to countries such as the two Irelands, Cypruses, and Palestines and the many Indias, is that conflict is the product of centuries-old hatreds between ethnically different groups who express their hatred in irrational forms of violence. Ethnic violence invites retaliation, which in turn leads to an endless spiral of violence. Writing about the Arab-Israeli conflict, for instance, journalist Marc Charney says, "In the West Bank, Gaza and Jerusalem, the conflict between Israeli and Palestinian is being shared by a fratricidal agony: competing, centuries-old claims to the same precious strip of land between the Jordan River and the Mediterranean, and the right to exist there as a nation. The rivalry is as old as the contest between Muslim and Jew for the legacy of their common father, Abraham" (1988). Much the same has been written about Hindus and Sikhs in India, Tamils and Sinhalese in Sri Lanka, Protestants and Catholics in Ireland, and Turks and Greeks in Cyprus.

A second argument typically given is that conflict in the divided states is a by-product of cold-war, superpower rivalry. In 1950, for instance, Dean Rusk, who would later become secretary of state under President Johnson, told the Senate Foreign Relations Committee that the war then raging between French colonialists and Viet Minh insurgents in Indochina was not simply a local struggle: "This is a civil war that has been in effect captured by the [Soviet] Politburo and . . . has been turned into a tool of the Politburo. So it isn't a civil war in the usual sense. It is part of an international war [between the United States and its allies and the Soviet Union and its allies]" (Karnow 1983, 179–80). This kind of explanation is usually applied to conflict between the two Koreas, Chinas, Vietnams, and Germanies, though one finds it cropping up in South Asia and the Middle East.

The first explanation assumes that the roots of conflict are indigenous and irrational; the second, that they are exogenous and calculating. From my study of devolution, partition, and war in the divided states, it is clear that both these explanations are wrong.

The first is wrong because these conflicts are not the product of centuries-old hatreds. The independence movements in these countries have a distinctly modern character, and conflicts between competing movements and states have contemporary roots that may be decades but not centuries old. These independence movements used parochial and cosmopolitan ideologies to organize the inhabitants of European colonies and set state power within the emerging interstate system as their goal. Both their ideologies and goals are modern. Organizers of these movements did not create them to conduct feuds and settle accounts, but to achieve citizenship in sovereign, secular states, which is a rational goal within the context of the modern interstate system.

The second is wrong because these conflicts are not a by-product of the cold war and superpower rivalry. The idea that inhabitants of the divided states would fight so bitterly for so long on behalf of the Kremlin or the White House is a superpower conceit. Superpower behavior during the course of conflict in the divided states cannot be adequately explained by their ostensible cold-war rivalry. Superpower interests are too often joined in the divided states. The superpowers acted in concert to divide these countries and, when conflict erupted in them, acted to confine and limit them in important ways. When push came to shove, inhabitants of the divided states found themselves abandoned or betrayed by their superpower allies, who might have been expected to conduct themselves in a cold-war manner, but did not.

The collective history of the divided states is complex, but it is important to explain why conflict in the divided states has relatively modern roots, why partition was advanced by the superpowers as a solution to the problems associated with the devolution of colonial or military power in these countries, and how partition, rather than solving outstanding political problems, created new ones that led to various kinds of war.

After World War II, revolutionary social movements throughout much of the world demanded an end to foreign military occupation and colonial rule. Because the war had transformed superpower relations, weakened colonial powers' ability to rule over transcontinental empires, and strengthened indigenous independence movements, the devolution of power to indigenous movements became a real possibility.

The independence movements that sought state power in the not-yet-divided states shared a number of features in common. First, they were relatively new social constructions. The older ones, such as the Indian National Congress and the Zionist movement, could trace their origins back to the late nineteenth century, but most were formed in the first decades of the twentieth century: Sinn Fein in 1905 and the Muslim League in 1906; nationalist and Communist parties in Korea, China, and Vietnam during the 1920s. Despite their short organizational life span, these movements all claimed much longer historical genealogies. The Vietnamese portrayed themselves as descendants of early nineteenth-century anticolonial movements; Zionists portrayed themselves as descendents of biblical Hebrew warriors. They invented these histories to establish themselves as legitimate claimants to power in a devolved state. But it is a mistake to take them at their word and say that they were really centuries-old movements.

Second, organizers of these movements used parochial and cosmopolitan ideologies to build "imagined communities," collectivities, sometimes called "nations," that could rightfully assume state power in an interstate system based on the nation-state. Common languages and religious and ethnic characteristics often comprised the parochial elements of organizer ideologies, but many of the organizing principles had exogenous origins that had to be imported. Nationalism does not necessarily begin at home. Movement organizers drew from cosmopolitan ideologies of nation and class to build their movements, and leaders of these movements developed political languages that could be spoken and understood in metropolitan capital and rural hamlet.

The language used by independence movements reflects their simultaneous cosmopolitan and parochial orientation. When addressing great and superpower authorities, movements spoke of the need for independence and self-determination. Thus when Ho Chi Minh announced the founding of a Communist republic in Hanoi in 1945, he cited a passage from the American Declaration of Independence to convey the cosmopolitan meaning of his act to metropolitan governments. The call for self-determination was also made because it conveyed a message that the superpowers could understand. Self-determination was a slogan advanced by U.S. president Woodrow Wilson and Bolshevik leader Vladimir Lenin to encourage the secession of colonial states from European empires. Mindful of this, movements in the colonies used the term to advance their claim for the devolution of power in Paris and London and to enlist the support of officials in Washington and Moscow.

But these movements spoke a different language of liberation in village and hamlet. When speaking to the indigenous inhabitants of their country, the Indian National Congress spoke of *swaraj*, the Viet Minh of *doc lap*, and Korean parties of *sinparam*. In the parochial idiom, these terms meant not independence or self-determination—the devolution of colonial power to indigenous successors and the creation of a sovereign state within the interstate system (abstract, sophisticated concepts)—but waking up, standing up for one's rights. *Doc lap*, for instance, means to "stand alone." *Sinparam*, in the words of the Korean writer Chong Kyong-mo, "expressed the pathos, the inner joy of a person moved to action not by coercion but by his own volition. *Param* is the sound of the wind; if a person is wafted along on this wind, songs burst from his lips and his legs dance with joy. A *sinparam* is a strange wind that billows in the hearts of people who have freed themselves from oppression, regained their freedom, and live in a society of mutual trust" (Cumings 1981, 68). Independence movements of necessity gave both cosmopolitan and parochial meaning to their struggle and spoke political languages that could be understood in London and Ahascragh or Bhiwandi or Ramala; Washington and Kyongju; Moscow and Pingxiang; and Paris and Nghi Loc.

Third, organizers of independence movements set state power as their goal. They believed that only state power would permit them to exercise fully their independence.

Social movements have not always set state power as their goal. The socialist movement only adopted it in the 1880s, after a lengthy debate between Anarchists and Marxists that precipitated the creation of the Second International. During the nineteenth and early twentieth centuries, state power was increasingly seen as a prerequisite of independence. It was the adoption of this goal that set Sinn Fein apart from predecessor movements, like that led by Parnell, or distinguished the Muslim League that met in Lahore in 1940 to demand a separate Moslem state from the Muslim League of the 1930s. It is a goal that separates reformist movements from revolutionary ones.

Fourth, most of these movements believed that violence, usually irregular war, was a necessary component of any strategy to achieve state power and independence. The Indian National Congress is alone among independence movements in the not-yet-divided states in its attempt to seize state power without resort to violence. The other movements were veterans of irregular and guerrilla war, though they did not practice it as the only means to their ends.

The devolution of political power in territories subject to colonial occupation and military rule was difficult for superpowers to manage. They had to determine how and to whom they should transfer power. As devolution approached, conflict between competing independence movements sharpened, and superpower devolvers were faced with the threat of civil war.

The simplest way to manage devolution under these circumstances would have been to transfer political power to the independence movement that could claim to represent a majority of people in a given territory. That would not have been difficult to determine, since in most cases one movement clearly commanded the loyalty of a large majority: Sinn Fein was supported by four-fifths of the Irish, the Indian National Congress by an overwhelming majority of Indians, and the Cypriot Independence party by nearly 80 percent of Cypriots. Communist parties in Korea, China, and Vietnam could claim substantial majorities. In Palestine, contending independence movements were more nearly balanced, and in Germany, indigenous movements, having been wiped out by the Nazis, were almost nonexistent.

But instead of awarding state power to majority movements, the various superpowers—Great Britain, France, the United States, and the Soviet Union—treated minorities as having an equal claim on power. This was done for ideological and practical reasons. At an ideological level, the equalization of movement claims was done to promote self-determination—the right of distinct nationalities to secede from empires and govern themselves—and prevent a tyranny of the majority from oppressing ethnic and ideological minorities. As a practical matter, it was done to reward friends and punish enemies.

In devolving power in British colonies such as Ireland and India, British administrators rewarded minority parties for their role in world wars. During World War I, Sinn Fein, the Irish Catholic majority party, agitated against the British war effort and even staged the abortive Easter Rebellion in 1916 to oust the British. Irish Protestants, meanwhile, rallied to the British war effort. During World War II, the majority Indian National Congress opposed mobilization for the war, while the minority Muslim League worked to defend the empire. Is it surprising, given this history, that the British would reward their wartime allies—minority independence movements—and punish majority independence movements that abandoned them during the war? As a reward, the British accorded loyal minority movements equal rights as devolution approached, and when these minority movements demanded state power on their own, the British moved toward partition as a solution.

In Asia, the story was a little different. In Korea and Vietnam, the United States, with Soviet consent, rearmed the collaborationist minority in order to check the power of Communist independence movements that had fought against the Japanese on the Allied side. In China, too, the United States and the Soviet Union quickly moved to support nationalist rule. In contrast to the British, the United States punished its erstwhile allies and rewarded wartime foes. But in the context of global superpower realignment, the United States acted to reward its future allies and punish future foes. It was this realignment that tipped the scales in favor of minority movements as devolution approached.

Having equalized unequal claims, the superpowers began to advance partition as a way to protect minority rights to self-determination. To accomplish this, they either practiced inventive cartographic gerrymandering—look, for instance, at the prepartition maps of India, Palestine, and Ireland—or simply drew a line across the territory at some convenient parallel. It is said that Dean Rusk labored only thirty minutes before deciding to draw a line demarcating U.S. and Soviet zones of occupation in Korea at the Thirty-Eighth Parallel. It took only a little more time for the superpowers to partition Vietnam at the Seventeenth Parallel.

As compensation for frustrating the aspirations of majority independence movements who wanted to assume power over a single, unified territory, the superpowers promised that partition would be a temporary expedient until tempers cooled, and they provided for reunification elections at some future date. The British provided for all-Irish, all-Indian, and all-Cypriot elections in devolution treaties. The United States and the Soviet Union promised to hold all-

Korean elections. All-German and all-Vietnamese elections were proposed but not adopted by all the superpower parties. As it turned out, only Cyprus ever held elections, and their results were undone by the Turkish invasion and partition of the island in 1974.

Instead of resolving the problems associated with devolution, partition created a number of new problems that compromised the meaning of citizenship and sovereignty in the divided states. Although partition was supposed to avert civil war, civil war erupted anyway, and civilian populations caught on the wrong side of the border fled. The scale of coerced and voluntary migration after partition is staggering. In India, for instance, 17 million people exchanged countries (Holland 1985, 80), and in Palestine, more than 900,000 Arab Palestinians fled to neighboring territories (Holland 1985, 121). This did not settle the matter. Huge residual populations remained behind—there are as many Moslems living in India today as reside in Pakistan.

The creation of separate states made majority populations minorities and minority populations majorities. Naturally, the presence of residual minority populations that had large, sympathetic populations living in neighboring states made state officials and nominal majorities extremely nervous. To secure their power, state authorities moved to disenfranchise minority populations, which were defined in ethnic terms in the ex-British colonies and in ideological terms in Korea, China, Vietnam, and Germany.

A survey of the divided states shows that in almost every one, authorities have moved against minority populations by enacting voting restrictions and passing laws restricting the right to intermarry, travel, buy or inherit land, perform military service and bear arms, practice religious observances, speak native languages, and demonstrate in public. Many states also subject minority populations to military or paramilitary rule. The results of efforts to consolidate majority rule are various systems of apartheid, which deny equal citizenship to inhabitants of the polity.

Not surprisingly, unequal treatment generates considerable hostility among disenfranchised populations and encourages them to reclaim their independence, often by force. The meaning of independence in this context differs. For some, it means secession, for others, it means reunification. But it always means a challenge to the authority of the state.

To obtain their independence, disenfranchised minorities often look to sympathetic populations in neighboring states for support. Because conflict can assume an external as well as an internal dimension, state officials view these challenges as threats to their sovereignty. Even without restive indigenous populations and threats from sibling states, sovereignty for the divided states is problematic. It has been extremely difficult for divided states to secure and maintain their sovereignty in the interstate system. The United States refused, for many years, to admit North Korea, China, or Vietnam to membership in the United Nations. Taiwan and Israel have both had their rights challenged in that body. Only Turkey has recognized North Kibris as an independent state, and the two Germanies were not accorded full recognition by the superpowers until the mid–1970s.

Because citizenship and sovereignty are partial and problematic, divided states attempt to remove the obstacles that prevent them from fully realizing each. All too often, the result is war. A few observations can be made about war in the divided states.

First, irregular war conducted by indigenous insurgents typically draws support from exogenous populations and states. This makes it very difficult for state officials to insolate and destroy insurgent guerrilla movements, and this tends to widen the war and invite intervention by neighboring and superpower states.

Second, just as it is difficult to confine participation in irregular wars to indigenous populations, it is difficult to restrict conventional wars to sibling states. Sibling states have superpower allies, which frequently intervene. It should be noted, however, that in almost every instance, these conventional wars are initiated by the divided states, usually without the consent or approval of their superpower allies. The superpowers may have helped create the conflicts in the divided states, but they do not control events in them. Divided states make their own trouble, which makes them troublesome for the superpowers. Wars in Korea, China, Vietnam, India, Pakistan, Israel, Cyprus, and Ireland have all been started by indigenous forces that have waged war on their own initiative.

For their part, the superpowers have acted to limit and confine these conflicts and prevent one side from winning conclusive victory. They usually act to maintain the status quo, which means continued partition. Only Vietnam has been reunified over superpower objections, and that took place only after twenty years of fighting.

Third, although the superpowers do not initiate irregular or conventional war, they regularly threaten to initiate nuclear war. Several things stand out in the history of covert superpower nuclear threats.

Most nuclear threats are made against nonnuclear opponents that could not respond in kind. The United States threatened North Korea, China, North Vietnam, East Germany, and the Soviet Union (during the first Berlin crisis) before those countries possessed nuclear weapons. This kind of behavior should not be particularly surprising since it is safer to threaten an unarmed adversary than an armed one.

When they have been threatened, the divided states have looked to their superpower ally, which has nuclear weapons, to deter or ward off nuclear threats. If the superpowers lived up to cold-war commitments or really practiced deterrence, they would risk nuclear war on behalf of their nonnuclear allies. But they have not. The Korean War and the Suez crisis of 1956 signalled to different sets of divided states the fact that the superpowers would not act to deter nuclear threats against their allies.

During the Korean War and subsequent Quemoy and Matsu crises (1950, 1953, and 1958), the Chinese and Koreans discovered that the Soviet Union could not or would not act to deter repeated U.S. nuclear threats even though the Soviet Union had recently acquired nuclear weapons. In 1963, Chinese foreign minister Chen Yi said of Soviet behavior: "How can any one nation say that they will defend another? These sort of promises are easy to make, but they are worth nothing. Soviet [nuclear] protection is worth nothing to us" (Kincade and Bertram 1982, 13). China exploded its own nuclear weapon one year later.

The Vietnamese discovered the same thing after being threatened by the United States during the war in Vietnam. As Stephen Kaplan says, "In the Korean War, the Quemoy and Cuban missile crises, the Vietnam War and the Sino-Vietnamese conflict, Moscow was more concerned about avoiding conflict with the United States and China than it was about protecting the sovereignty and security of its allies, who, if they may not have expected the Soviet Union to go to war on their behalf, did seem to expect the Kremlin to do more than it did" (1981, 241).

U.S. allies discovered much the same thing in 1956. When the British, French, and Israelis unilaterally seized the Suez Canal from Soviet-supported Egypt, the Soviets threatened to use nuclear weapons to dislodge them. The United States refused to support its allies in their confrontation with the Soviet Union, and they were forced to withdraw. This development prompted both France and Israel to develop their own nuclear forces. Whether developed by Communist China, nonaligned India, Moslem Pakistan, or Jewish Israel, the *force de frappe* became the generic response to U.S.-Soviet nuclear threats.

Some semblance of stability and deterrence has resulted from superpower nuclear parity, but the acquisition of nuclear weapons by some of the divided states cannot be said to have had the same effect. The acquisition of nuclear weapons in this context—where states are prone to war, where the acquisition of nuclear weapons by sibling states is seen as a direct threat to a country's survival as a state, and where the norm of international behavior is to use or threaten to use nuclear weapons against nonnuclear opponents or against opponents that have decisively inferior nuclear forces—is an extremely dangerous development.

Partition, a political solution to problems associated with the devolution of power in states subject to military occupation or colonial rule, was supposed to lead to self-determination. It has led instead to disenfranchisement, apartheid, and war. It has also led to subdivision: Pakistan was subdivided in 1971 when a secessionist movement in East Pakistan, with Indian assistance, broke away from Pakistan during a fearsome civil war to create Bangladesh. Despite its obvious failings, it is still being applied as a solution to problems around the world: Lebanon, Sri Lanka, and Ethiopia are all candidates for superpower partition in coming years. The historical record suggests that self-determination does not lead toward democracy, but away from it.

Self-determination may have been appropriate in the context of empire and colony, where it meant independence, or the right to secede from colonial rule. But in the context of the interstate system, where nation-states, not colonies, are the rule, self-determination acquires a different meaning. It enables ruling majorities to reject interference in sovereign affairs even though the inhabitants of neighboring states have a stake in those affairs, and it legitimizes the claims of disenfranchised minorities to secede from the polity that oppresses them even though they may in turn impose their rule on a dissenting minority within a newly created state. As Abraham Lincoln said of the right to secession, "If a minority will secede rather than acquiesce, they make a precedent which in turn will divide and ruin them; for a majority of their own will secede from them whenever a majority refuses to be controlled by such a minority" (Sandburg 1939, 132). In the divided states, it is difficult to see how the pursuit of self-determination by majorities and minorities will lead to democracy, and without democracy there is no way to resolve the social and political problems that divide them.

NOTES

1. This work is based on my book, *Warpaths: The Politics of Partition*. New York: Hill and Wang, 1990.
2. There is some disagreement over the number of times the United States and the Soviet Union have threatened to use nuclear weapons. The number depends on the definition of "threat." But while the totals may vary, the proportions do not. That is, whatever definition is used, divided states are still subject to the majority of threats.

REFERENCES

Betts, Richard K. 1987. *Nuclear Blackmail and Nuclear Balance*. Washington, D.C.: Brookings Institution.
Blechman, Barry, and Stephen Kaplan. 1978. *Force without War*. Washington, D.C.: Brookings Institution.
Charney, Marc. 1988. *New York Times*, February 28.
Cumings, Bruce. 1981. *The Origins of the Korean War*. Princeton: Princeton University Press.
Ellsberg, Daniel. 1981. "Call to Mutiny." In *Protest and Survive*, edited by Edward Thompson and Dan Smith, i–xxviii. New York: Monthly Review Press.
Halperin, Morton. 1987. *Nuclear Fallacy*. Cambridge, Mass.: Ballinger.
Holland, R. F. 1985. *European Decolonization, 1918–1981*. New York: St. Martin's Press.
Kaplan, Stephen. 1981. *Diplomacy of Power*. Washington, D.C.: Brookings Institution.
Karnow, Stanley. 1983. *Vietnam: A History*. New York: Viking Press.
Kincade, William, and Christopher Bertram. 1982. *Nuclear Proliferation in the 1980s*. London: MacMillan.
Sandburg, Carl. 1939. *Abraham Lincoln: The War Years*. Vol. 1. New York: Harcourt, Brace.
Schaeffer, Robert. 1990. *Warpaths: The Politics of Partition*. New York: Hill and Wang.
Sivard, Ruth L. 1987. *World Military and Social Expenditures, 1987–88*. Washington, D.C.: World Priorities.

8

ECONOMIC FLUCTUATIONS, MILITARY EXPENDITURES, AND WARFARE IN INTERNATIONAL RELATIONS

Raimo Väyrynen

Economic fluctuations, power transitions, and military spending are historically interlinked. Furthermore, they all are associated in a complex manner with the frequency and severity of wars between major powers. This chapter does not purport to trace the decision making behind arms races and outbreaks of wars, but rather to place them in a structural, historical context. I will pay particular attention to the critical variables describing this context, that is, the long waves of economic development and power transitions between major states. There is no simple relationship between these two structural variables, but they are assumed to have independent effects on the extent and nature of arms races and warfare.

Long waves and power transitions have a dual character. They are both explanatory variables in a traditional sense and a means of periodizing the historical reality. Periodization helps to ascertain whether the turning points in economic cycles or in the power-transition processes engender qualitative changes in international relations.

The reliance on economic cycles and power transitions in structuring the argument brings together two different and perhaps even incompatible approaches. Economic cycles reflect the development logic of the world economy and can only in part be reduced to the performance of individual national economies. Power transitions have a more statecentric focus in which major powers figure prominently. It is a bone of contention among international relations scholars whether power transitions can be described as a systemic process as well. In any case, one methodological problem is the relationship between the state and systemic levels of analysis.

Given the long time period from the middle of the nineteenth century to the present, the number of structural factors considered, and the number of states covered, the conclusions are bound to be incomplete. I will suggest a number of tentative historical relationships and provide a sketch and a framework for further analysis. Such a framework can only be validated by more focused studies of individual cases and comparisons of them. Historical material introduced in this chapter is intended to illustrate the general observations rather than to prove them.

LONG WAVES

Historically, economic constraints have shaped the level and intensity of military efforts. Without a sufficient military-industrial base, domestic development and procurement of arms are not possible. Advanced civilian and military technologies of each historical period are controlled by a few leading corporations of the core states. The more advanced the technology, the fewer the number of states and corporations that can gain access to it. From these centers, weapons systems and military technologies have radiated, through the tranfers of arms and military technologies, to semiperipheral and peripheral countries. The concentration of control in the world military order is fostered by the leadership in military research and development, which is pivotal for technological innovations. If the leading military powers are unable to stay at the edge of military innovations, their commanding position will soon be eroded.

The acquisition of national military power is constrained by the position of a state in the global core-periphery structure. The core powers have quantitatively larger and qualitatively more diverse military establishments. Such states may escape, by a policy decision, from the heavy military burden, but they seldom do. The economic resources of small states, in turn, are so scarce that they are never able to acquire a military potential that could match the military capabilities of leading states. The military inequality of core and peripheral states is a central feature of the global political system.

The core-periphery structure shapes the distribution of military capabilities between states (for evidence, see Neumann 1984). This structure is historically transformed by recurrent economic cycles and the transitions of power between leading states. Long waves of capitalist development, or Kondratieff cycles, are directly related to the acquisition of military capabilities. During the boom phase of the long cycle, national economies prosper and funds accumulate in the state coffers that may be used to support internal and external military expansion. During these phases, states are able to increase their military capabilities, which are justified by the need for national prowess and external expansion.

Recently there has been much debate about the existence and timing of Kondratieff cycles. Over time, the lines of debate have converged. There is empirical support for the claim that there are long-term periodicities in the world-economy, both in prices and in economic activity. The periodicities are more consistent in the price data than in the production data (Goldstein 1988, 67–98). The nature of such periodicities differs from one national economy to another, and they are not necessarily uniform, as Kondratieff suggested. Kondratieff cycles are obviously too mechanical to provide a basis for a theory of international economic and political dynamics. As a consequence, Kondratieff's conception of uniform development patterns needs to be modified (Beenstock 1983, 137–59; Menzel 1985).

Without putting too much of a theoretical premium on long cycles, they can be used to periodize world economic dynamics. In this connection, it will suffice to repeat the standard periodization of the downswing and the upswing phases of the cycle. The periods 1815–1850, 1873–1897, 1920–1945, and from 1967 on are downswings, while the remaining periods of 1850–1873, 1897–1914, and 1945–1967 are upswings. World War I has sometimes been annexed to the preceding upswing and World War II to the following upswing, and the beginning of the most recent downswing has sometimes been timed to 1973 rather than to 1967 (Goldstein 1988, 67). This periodization should be considered as a tool of analysis rather than as the last word in economic time-series analysis. Empirical descriptions of economic cycles and transitions are indispensable, but only theoretical explications of the causes of such economic transitions can make the analysis of their political and military correlates meaningful (Kleinknecht 1981).

POWER TRANSITIONS

The model of power transitions rests on the primacy of domestic economic, technological, and institutional factors in the generation of economic growth and expansion. International power transitions result, in the first place, from the internal dynamics of national economies and polities. The structure of the international system has an important and variable role in enabling and constraining the growth of national economies within the system. The variable impact of the international structure is reflected in the differential opportunities of peripheral and core nations for economic gain. This is also the case with the historical development of core powers.

The United States, for example, rose to the core of the world economy as a result of indigenous industrial dynamics, relatively free of international constraints. British economic and naval supremacy, on the other hand, was predicated on political and military equilibrium on the European continent. The U.S. experience does not mean that the international system does not impinge on domestic development. The issue is "not whether the international system shapes domestic politics, but how and through what mechanisms" (Gourevitch 1986, 65). In the U.S. case, the South's dependence on the European market for cotton sales helped to pave the way for the Civil War (Keohane 1983).

Recently the dynamics of ascending and declining hegemonies has provided a popular framework for the analysis of international power cycles and power transitions. Particular attention has been paid to the role of industrialization and deindustrialization in the rise and decline of economic and military capabilities (Organski 1964, 300–306). The rise and decline of states has to be understood in relative terms, that is, in relation to other rising and declining powers. Decline is also caused by internal and external developments in the leading power itself. Leading powers suffer from economic and institutional slack, the overextension of civilian and military bureaucracy, and, overall, from diminishing returns from their international positions (Gilpin 1981).

Power transitions generate conflicts between nations whose relative international positions are simultaneously changing. In particular, conflicts of interest between rising and declining powers tend to escalate into military crises and confrontations, as various theories of hegemonic war have intermittently stressed. The fixation with military war as the dominant mechanism of international change, however, overlooks the economic aspect of competition, which is reflected, among other things, in the economic costs of military competition associated with the processes of power transition. It is no novel observation that the military burden becomes a costly drain on national resources and tests the economic endurance of nations; it is "one of the crucial tests in the struggle for existence." Competition in economic endurance may develop into a substitute for war that "ruins states and crushes nations" and "is waged without firing a shot" (van Dyke Robinson 1900, 619–22).

Empirically, world-system analysts argue that in its hegemonic ascent during the Napoleonic Wars, Great Britain experienced hegemonic victory during the downswing of 1815–1850 and enjoyed hegemonic maturity during the upswing of 1850–1873. After the decline of British hegemony in 1897–1914, the United States embarked upon a similar cycle from the upswing of 1897–1914 on: U.S. hegemonic victory occurred between the two world wars, culminating in its hegemonic maturity between 1945 and 1967. Since then, the United States has experienced a gradual decline in its hegemony (Hopkins and Wallerstein 1979; Väyrynen 1983, 395–402).

The world-system approach pairs the phases of Kondratieff cycles with those of the hegemonic development. The transition toward unicentricity is assumed to occur during the upswing phase of the long economic cycle. The return to multicentricity, characterized by intense political and economic conflicts, takes place during the economic downturn (Bousquet 1980, 48–50). For theoretical purposes, the establishment of an analytical linkage between the long waves of economic development and the international power cycle may be justified, but for empirical purposes, it is important to keep them analytically separate.

The process of economic power transition before World War I can be illustrated by the distribution of gross national product (GNP) among the major powers (table 8.1). The economic power transition before World War I saw the rise of the United States and the fall of Great Britain. However, Britain's decline was relatively slow during the last two decades of the nineteenth century, and its international position still had many strengths. But it faced too many simultaneous challenges from too many major powers to be able to retain its predominance

Table 8.1
Distribution of Economic Resources (GNP) among the Major Powers, 1870–1913
(Percentages)

	1870	1880	1890	1900	1913
Russia	19.8	19.1	17.7	17.1	16.9
USA	19.6	26.1	28.2	30.6	36.0
UK	19.3	17.5	19.3	17.8	14.3
France	17.8	15.6	14.1	12.8	10.3
Germany	16.8	16.3	15.7	16.4	17.0
Japan	6.7	5.4	5.0	5.3	5.5
Total	100.0	100.0	100.0	100.0	100.0

Source: Kugler and Organski 1986, 10.

(Kennedy 1987, 224–32). These challenges emanated especially from the United States, but also from Germany and Russia. In 1870, the challengers were equal. During the following decades, Germany and Russia lost the race for economic predominance to the United States, but defeated Great Britain. France experienced the most rapid fall of economic standing in relation to other major powers.

The same picture emerges from an analysis of the distribution of the production of manufactured goods and iron and steel. The only visible deviation is the much more rapid rise of Germany's heavy industry than of its economic potential in general (Kennedy 1984). Germany's industrial breakthrough occurred in two waves of technological innovations, which coincided with two upswings of the long economic cycles (Trebilcock 1981, 48–50). The recovery phase of the latter upswing in 1883–1892 was characterized by a high rate of basic innovations, particularly in the United States and Germany (van Duijn 1983, 180–85).

Technological innovations and industrialization also reshaped the European power structure. States failing to achieve broad-based industrialization, such as France and Russia, lost their chance to become hegemonic states. Industrial development "made wealth and industrial capacity the decisive factor in international power" (Hobsbawm 1979, 84–85). The limited scope of the U.S. external expansion made the international political and military bearing of its economic potential smaller than it would have been otherwise. In Europe, the situation was different because Germany did not hesitate to use its economic prowess to advance expansionist ends. That is why "the industrialization of Germany was a major historical fact" (Hobsbawm 1979, 40).

The gathering economic competition between Britain and Germany was not felt in political and military fields before the beginning of the twentieth century. Until then, continental European powers did not challenge the British colonial position. In the absence of serious challenge, Britain had an opportunity to deal with colonial rebellions one by one, without interference by other colonial powers

(Porter 1983, 44–45). But the Boer War demonstrated that the British ability to govern rebellious colonies was fading.

Hegemonic decline also contributed to the British policy of concluding an alliance with Japan in 1902. The alliance was primarily intended to contain Russian expansion in the Far East, but it also recognized Japan's economic and military interests on the Asian mainland. The agreement was "a stage in the working out of Japanese imperialism" (Beasley 1987, 76–77). After the Russo-Japanese War, Britain sought to reach an understanding with Russia to end their rivalry, the "great game," by agreeing on spheres of influence in Asia. To this effect, a Russo-British convention was concluded in 1907 to complement a similar agreement between Russia and Japan.

It has been pointed out that these agreements, in effect, marked the end of the "great game" because the British perceptions of international rivalries had changed. This change meant that the British policy focused on the "growing power of Germany and the naval and imperial ambitions of its emperor as likely to constitute in the future the central threat to British security. It was a threat which would have to be neutralized by the British throwing their weight against Germany in the European balance of power" (Gillard 1977, 170–71). Such an orientation had been brewing for years in the nationalist press and political opinion in Britain, which became, in the early 1900s, increasingly hostile toward Germany (Kennedy 1982, 255–65).

The power transition process led to conflict between Great Britain and Germany. Britain made efforts to arrest its decline by aligning with Japan and France and by regulating its competition with Russia. As the dominant maritime power, Britain tried to prevent the leading land powers, Germany and Russia, from joining forces. Britain was able to prevent a German-Russian alliance, but it could not maintain peace and stability on the continent. World War I broke out, devastated Europe, and transformed postwar international relations. This transformation was felt in several different ways.

World War I catalyzed social and political revolutions in Russia and Germany, which removed them temporarily from a position of power. The war contributed to the dissolution of the Austro-Hungarian Empire and the rise of a cluster of small states. The United States decided to withdraw to a semi-isolationist policy. It profited from war without having to experience its destructiveness and gained access to new markets. After the war, the United States was the most powerful country in the world, which enabled it to wield a kind of veto power over British influence on international relations. But the United States did not effectively use this power. Instead, it permitted Great Britain to regain much of its previous power position. In other words, "Britain was given a further lease of life as a world power," even though the resurrection was temporary and bound to last only until its rivals recovered and the United States returned from self-imposed isolation (Porter 1983, 84–86).

The redistribution of economic resources since World War I among the major powers is illustrated in table 8.2. Until the 1930s, Germany and the Soviet Union

Table 8.2
Distribution of Economic Resources (GNP) among the Major Powers, 1925–1980
(Percentages)

USA	42.5	36.3	50.0	42.5	40.7	36.6
USSR	15.1	20.8	20.1	24.8	21.5	21.8
UK	12.6	11.7	10.6	8.6	6.3	5.4
Germany	12.2	15.0	7.1	9.2	11.6	11.2
France	9.6	7.0	7.2	7.1	8.6	8.2
Japan	8.0	9.2	5.0	7.8	11.3	16.8
Total	100.0	100.0	100.0	100.0	100.0	100.0

Source: Kugler and Organski 1986, 10.

were weak. This situation began to change in the 1930s. As a consequence of the Great Depression in 1929–1933, the United States, Great Britain, and France suffered from a decline in their relative economic standing. At the same time, forced industrialization in the Soviet Union, the alliance between state power and big companies in Nazi Germany, and the coalition between military bureaucrats and the *zaibatsu* in Japan captured a greater share of economic resources for challenging states. These countries based their economic expansion on autarky, which worked as a short-term strategy but also increased the need for external expansion. The shift in relative power positions of the revisionist and status quo powers undermined the political order created for Europe at Versailles.

Autarky and the international conflicts of the 1930s, which were initiated by the revisionist powers, destroyed the international division of labor. In Britain, the decline of its economic hegemony, the slow rate of innovation in basic industries, and the Great Depression contributed to the General Tariff of 1932 and the abandonment of free trade. The British iron and steel industry demanded more protection against external competition from the United States and Germany (Capie 1983, especially 63–75). Japan and Germany made rearmament a political priority. Economic policy was subordinated to rearmament once it became clear that resources were inadequate to pursue both. In Germany, the crisis of governance resulted in the late 1930s in the restoration of Nazi control over the economy and the military (Deist 1981; Geyer 1984, 144–53).

In the middle of the 1930s, international relations were polarized between the revisionist and status quo states, and preparations for war were well under way. In both groups, military spending helped overcome the economic depression. Eugen Varga perceptively predicted that a general war and an economic crisis were approaching. The German, Italian, and Japanese autarky undermined international cooperation and overburdened their economies with huge investments in war preparations (1935, 122–38).

The resulting domestic instabilities increased the need for external expansion.

This development was facilitated in Germany by the military's professional confusion. Procurement decisions, deployment plans, and operational details became the main preoccupation of the military, which was unable to develop a coherent strategy to guide the acquisition and use of military hardware. The military's inability to develop a sound strategic framework for armaments policy had devastating international consequences. It also helped Hitler to take over the leadership of military affairs. His military policy precipitated, and the economic crisis of 1938–1939 accelerated, the plunge into a global war (Geyer 1984, 149–53; Geyer 1985).

The system of collective security, written in the Covenant of the League of Nations, was neither collective nor secure. Its maintenance was the responsibility of Great Britain and France. Britain, a declining power, preferred peace and practiced appeasement, while France put more emphasis on military rearmament (Porter 1983, 96–98). British policy was ineffective because it failed to deter German expansionism, and French policy failed because it lacked economic resources to back up its threats. The Axis powers might have been deterred by the Allied powers acting in concert in the late 1930s. Germany's expansionist policy worked only so long as it was able to attack its adversaries one by one (Kugler and Domke 1986, 63–65). The Battle of Britain, the attack on the Soviet Union, and the U.S. decision to join the war made German defeat almost inevitable. The only real question was how long the victory by the Allied powers would take to achieve.

The United States was again able to benefit from the war by enhancing its productive capacity and by conquering new markets during and after the war. U.S. hegemonic maturity after the war was due both to its own strength and to the weakness of other major powers. In that regard, the U.S. position did not appreciably differ from the experiences of the previous economic powers. The economic recovery of Japan and Germany increased their share of economic resources in the six-power system from 12.1 percent in 1950 to 28.0 percent in 1980. The relative economic power of the United States and of Great Britain has declined since the 1950s.

The power competition after World War II differs from that of previous periods in that it has not been primarily economic. In economic terms, the Soviet Union has been losing rather than winning this rivalry, and as a consequence, competition between the capitalist powers has been deferred. The coming process of power transition appears to be more economic than military. The new complexity of international relations places a premium on economic and technological resources and reduces the opportunities to wield military force effectively.

LONG WAVES AND WARFARE

The focus on the long waves of economic development and its political and military correlates contains an assumption that there are periodicities in the occurrence of international warfare. After examining empirical evidence, Singer and Gusack conclude that it "does not support the cyclical view" of the occurrence of war. It is quite possible, however, that "war requires the concatenation of several conditions, each of whose appearance is cyclical, but with different intervals" (1981, 410). This justifies an exploration of the relative contributions of long waves and power transitions to the explanation of major-power warfare.

In such an exploration, there are two possible research strategies. In the empirical approach the occurrence of general wars is measured independently of their structural consequences in the international system. This approach aims to find the causes of major wars and the mechanism by which they lead to the outbreak of large-scale violence (Levy 1985, 359–60). In the theoretical approach, whether based on world-system analysis or political realism, general wars are analyzed in the context of macrohistorical changes. Such changes qualitatively transform the economic and political structure of international relations. In this case, general war is not an empirical concept and does not have much meaning in isolation from the proper theoretical context. Various methodological problems notwithstanding, general wars are defined by their consequences for the system structure. They are often regarded even as the critical turning points, "benchmark wars," in the process of systemic change (for example, Thompson and Rasler 1986).

Forms of Warfare

In the empirical tradition, the study of the economic dynamics underpinning major-power wars would be based either on long waves or on various phase periods. In both cases, a reasonable assumption is that general wars are associated with economic turning points, either preceding or following them. Before dwelling upon the discussion of this assumption, one has to explore how the concept of war should be operationalized. In this regard, one can focus either on the forms of warfare or on the causes of war. In the former case, the main issue is the military, technological, or political character of war. One solution to the definition and periodization of war is that proposed by Michael Mann (1987): limited war (1648–1914), citizen warfare (1915–1945), and nuclear war (1945–). These characterizations of different types of war may be compared with Hans Speier's (1969) three categories of absolute, instrumental, and agonistic wars, or with Michael Howard's (1976) categories of professional, revolutionary, national, and technological wars.

Historical forms of warfare may be dealt with by combining these three perspectives in the following manner. In the eighteenth century, warfare was instrumental, but limited, in part for logistical reasons, and did not approach the ferocity of absolute warfare. This period was followed by a hiatus of revolutionary warfare, primarily by France, based on national mobilization and challenge to the European status quo. The pendulum swung back after 1815; the national aspect of warfare was controlled by the Concert of Europe and its instrumentality hedged by fear of social revolution. The dominant form of warfare was limited and primarily intended to quell antisystem revolts in the emerging nations of Europe.

After 1870, the limited nature of international warfare was complemented by new developments that culminated in World War I. Industrial capacity and technological innovation became the hallmarks of military power, increasing its mobility, flexibility, and destructiveness. Technological revolution in warfare, having an impact on both land and sea, had two conflicting effects. On the one hand, it enhanced the instrumental character of war; a reversion occurred to "war as a normal instrument of policy by governments who now ceased to believe that it must be avoided for fear of consequent revolution, and who were also rightly convinced that the power-mechanism was capable of keeping them within limits" (Hobsbawm 1979, 83).

On the other hand, industrial warfare required the mobilization of national economic and human resources in order to prevail in a total confrontation with an adversary. Mobilization imposed heavy burdens on citizens and activated most of the population for a common military effort. In that sense, total war was also a national war. Technological innovation contributed to the mobility of war, but at the same time, the totalization of war also increased the possibility of a prolonged and stalemated military confrontation, a war of attrition between industrial capacities of states (Howard 1976, 111–15). Blitzkrieg and trench warfare are two contradictory aspects of the same phenomenon, the totalization of war.

World War I transformed warfare by leading to the maturation of some earlier developments, such as the growing role of technology and nationalism. The end of World War I did not lead to a divorce in the marriage between the military force and the productive forces. On the contrary, the marriage was strengthened by the incorporation of new elements, such as air power. In that sense, World War II was a replay of the 1914–1918 conflict rather than a novel phenomenon. The critical difference was the invention of the atomic bomb and its instrumental use against Japan. The totalization of war, however, was reaching its absolute limits. With the proliferation of nuclear weapons, the instrumental use of new destructive power became increasingly difficult to conceive.

The relationship between changing forms of warfare and the long economic cycles is tenuous, although some connections may be pointed out. Obviously, the limited and instrumental nature of warfare from the Congress of Vienna to the Crimean War was associated both with the prevalence of a conservative policy of order and economic stagnation. Instruments of land warfare did not develop much during this period. While a transition from sail to steam occurred in the navies, their operations were limited to coastal defense. The imperial implications of steam, demanding coaling stations and naval bases, became manifest only later in the nineteenth century (Pearton 1982, 53–58).

After the middle of the nineteenth century, military technologies changed rapidly. There are two competing explanations of this development in weapons technology. It may have been released by the Crimean War, as McNeill (1982, 232–37) suggests, or it may have been spurred by the economic upswing of 1850–1872 and associated technological innovations. The first railway boom, revolutionizing land warfare, occurred during this upswing. It was associated with the rise of the steel industry as the leading sector in the international economy. Railways were multifunctional. They were used to pioneer industrial development, unite nations, and conduct military operations.

If the Crimean War was the last preindustrial war, the Franco-Prussian War of 1870–1871 may be considered the first major industrial war between states. In that war, "the successful application of technique in the form of the railway for mobilizing and concentrating armies, and the telegraph and telephone for controlling their operations, removed the two greatest restrictions on the effective deployment of manpower in war" (Pearton 1982, 101). The transformation of strategy by new means of communication was accompanied in the 1850s and the 1860s by organizational reforms and breakthroughs in weapons technologies, in particular firearms and artillery (Howard 1976, 97–103; McNeill 1982, 248–55).

The economic slowdown after the early 1870s may have delayed somewhat the technological transformation of warfare, but its impact remained limited. Long-term economic growth was only slightly affected in Germany and the United States, which were centers of military innovations. Furthermore, in the development of productive forces, the carryover effects from the previous upswing were so robust that the technological innovation in warfare did not stop. Transformation in warfare was a long-term tendency that was affected but not directed by ups and downs of the long economic cycle.

A new upswing after the early 1890s was needed to finalize a major change in the form of warfare. During this upswing, both naval capabilities and strategies were deeply transformed by technological innovations, in particular in command technology (McNeill 1982, 278–81). On land, further improvements in transport and communication enabled the formulation of new military strategies, such as the Schlieffen Plan in Germany (Pearton 1982, 125–31). Various wars in the Balkans, the Far East, and South Africa reinforced the lessons of the Franco-Prussian wars about the crucial importance of well-equipped infantry to repel assaulting forces (Howard 1976, 104–5).

The relatively low level of military spending and military innovation in the 1920s and the early 1930s may be accounted for both by slow economic growth and the absence of intense rivalries between major powers. The situation changed in the middle of the 1930s, when leading states, afflicted by the Great Depression, adopted expansionist policies. In this context, the "pace of improvement in weapons design, having slowed down drastically at the end of World War I, suddenly accelerated, especially for airplanes and tanks" (McNeill 1982, 350).

The intensification of power rivalries in the 1930s may have been the decisive factor in fueling military innovation. The economic upswing before World War II only provided resources needed to back up political decisions. Similarly, it may be that the unprecedented military buildup after World War II was made possible by rapid economic expansion. However, the real motivating force behind the arms race was the bipolar military and ideological competition between the United States and the Soviet Union. The development of new technologies at large has been influenced not only by demand in the civilian market, but by military requirements as well (Sen 1984).

There is some evidence that long economic cycles, which regulate the availability of resources, have shaped the rate of technological innovations and their military applications. It is more doubtful to suggest that the dynamics of long economic cycles are able to account for changes in the nature of warfare, but some connections remain. There is plenty of evidence that technological innovations underpinning transformations in warfare are associated with long periods of economic expansion and decline (van Duijn 1983, 129–43). In that way, long economic cycles have an indirect impact on military technology as well. On the other hand, there are may secular trends in technological development that continue independently of the economic cycles.

Another possibility is that transformations in the forms of warfare are associated with the phase periods of capitalist economic development rather than with the Kondratieff cycles. Angus Maddison, for instance, rejects the claims that there are recurrent long-term cycles in economic development. Rather, the transition from one phase period to another is "caused by system-shocks," which are "specific disturbances of an ad hoc character" (Maddison 1982, 83). In this analysis, the turning points of capitalist development occurred in 1913 and 1950. Maddison is less certain whether similar turning points occurred in 1870 and 1973.

Other authors have characterized the period from the Napoleonic Wars to about 1870 as an era of irresistibly rising industrialism and deepening sociopolitical polarization. During the trend period of 1870 to 1914, industrialization continued, but was accompanied by vigorous imperial expansion. The third trend period extends from 1914 to 1945–1950. During this period, the two world wars reorganized international relations and paved the way for a new trend period. Since World War II, capitalism has become truly internationalized under the aegis of transnational banks and corporations (Beaud 1981).

Maddison's phase periods are somewhat difficult to use in an analysis of changing warfare because wars themselves are major system shocks assumed to bring about the turning points. This problem notwithstanding, the phase-period model, which is not empirically incompatible with the cycle model, may be relevant in explaining changes in the nature of warfare. If 1914 and 1945 are considered to be the critical turning points in capitalist development, a correlation with the transformation in warfare appears.

World War I signified the unprecedented totalization of warfare. It was both a technological and nationalist war. The transformation brought about by nuclear weapons was of less consequence because it did not initiate any novel trend, but rather perfected the totalization process. The consideration of 1914 and 1945 as critical turning points is compatible with Mandelbaum's suggestion (1981, 17–20) that a mechanical revolution, the large-scale use of machines in warfare, culminated in World War I, while the nuclear revolution was fostered by World War II. An important difference between these two transformations was that in the mechanical revolution defense prevailed, while the nuclear revolution augmented the primacy of the offensive.

Maddison himself is uncertain whether 1870 signified a turning point in the phase periods of capitalist development. In military technology and form of warfare, there were hardly any crucial changes around this time. The profound impact of industrialization on military technology and warfare became visible before 1870 and continued as a secular trend, that culminated in World War I. In this context, the relevance of the Krondratieff cycles has to be recognized: the economic upswings of 1850–1872 and 1897–1914 pushed forward military-industrial innovations and their use in warfare. In the middle of the 1930s, a general improvement in economic activity permitted an upsurge in weapons acquisitions. In all these cases, the motivating forces were connected with political-military rivalries between states, and the new economic resources permitted rather than dictated the militarization process.

The Occurrence of Wars

Opinion is divided about the ability of long waves to account for the outbreak of wars. There is evidence for a fifty-year cycle in the occurrence of great-power wars. These cycles peak in a high-fatality war between great powers preceded by a series of wars of escalating severity. War peaks in 1870 (the Franco-Prussian War) and 1915 (World War I) differ from other peaks in that these wars were shorter and were not preceded by a spiral of escalating wars. Compared with earlier centuries, the period from the Napoleonic Wars to the twentieth century has more peace years, and war peaks are of shorter duration. This historical trend suggests that after 1945 even fewer great-power wars will take place, but if they occur, destruction will be very severe. The effects of nuclear weapons on warfare yield a similar picture of the present nature of warfare.

World War II is the deviating case in the cyclical pattern because it started too soon after the 1914 war. World War II is also exceptional in another respect. The other war peaks occur toward the end of an economic upswing, while World War II started a new upswing (Goldstein 1988, 239–43). Other studies tend to corroborate the observation that wars between great powers break out during the economic upswing, and even more importantly, that after 1815 no such wars have been started during a depression. Wars between great powers occur during periods of economic expansion, while stagnation hinders their outbreak (Väyrynen 1983, 410–11; see also Thompson and Zuk 1982, 622–24).

The results are different if all the wars involving great powers during a longer time span are considered. Such wars are distributed quite evenly between different phases of long waves. This concerns only the number of wars, not their severity.

Wars breaking out during the economic upswings are much more fatal than those starting during the downswings (Goldstein 1988, 245–49). This suggests that expansion and innovation in the economy, characteristic of an upswing, increase the destructiveness of warfare, but do not affect the probability of a war breaking out. An implication of this finding is that economic cycles and phase periods have more influence on the technological conditions of warfare than on their occurrence.

There seems to be a more direct relationship between economic cycles and the involvement of major powers in peripheral wars. Military interventions in peripheral societies have been associated with the expansion of world capitalism and the incorporation of new areas into the world-economy. As a rule, the core-periphery wars embody repression by the dominant actor and efforts at emancipation by the weaker party. Not only does the economic upswing generate new resources to wage wars, but expansion also creates political frictions within peripheries leading to wars (Hobsbawm 1979, 81–83; Väyrynen 1983, 411–12). In core-periphery wars, the superior military organization and technology of the colonial powers, which destroyed indigenous peoples and their conditions for living, usually prevailed (Headrick 1981, 115–26).

POWER TRANSITIONS AND WARFARE

The standard version of the power-transition model claims that major wars break out between the dominant or hegemonic power and its main challenger. It assumes that the "propensity to international conflicts is likely to increase as soon as the predominant political position of a once hegemonic power tends to decrease relatively (Senghaas 1983, 119). On the other hand, the challengers have accumulated material resources, but are dissatisfied with the way in which costs and benefits are distributed by the existing international order. Such dissatisfaction tends to foster war: "The major wars of recent history have all been wars involving the biggest power in the world and its allies against a challenger (or group of challengers) who have recently risen in power thanks to industrialization (Organski 1964, 322–23).

The hypothesis that power transitions create a zone of friction that increases the possibility of war has been empirically scrutinized and confirmed. Kugler and Organski (1980, 49–63) show that the differences in economic growth rates, which favor the challenger, lead to increased warfare. A similar conclusion has been reached by Thompson (1983, 103–11), although he is critical of the research techniques used by Kugler and Organski. Equally critical of them are Houweling and Siccama (1988), but they arrive at a similar result on the positive correlation between the power-transition process and the outbreak of wars. They extend this correlation to the entire category of major powers and not only to the group of dominant powers.

Before the power-transition model is accepted as a superior explanation of the occurrence of war, some caveats have to be made. Power transitions do not always lead to warfare between great powers. At times when one power is overtaking the other, war breaks out in about half of the cases and does not break out in the other half (Houweling and Siccama 1988, 101). The transfer of world leadership from Great Britain to the United States without an armed conflict between the two is a remarkable example of the peaceful transfer of power (Organski 1964, 323–25).

Another caveat is that major wars are not initiated by the leading economic challenger, as the primitive version of the power-transition theory suggests, but by a secondary contender. Otherwise, World War I would have been waged between the United States and Great Britain, and World War II would have started at the outset between the United States and Germany. Geographical proximity, the military emphasis in the German *Weltpolitik*, and incompatibilities in their sociopolitical orders all help to explain why the main contention in Europe before World War I occurred between Germany and Great Britain.

A geopolitical approach may be useful in explaining why the reality deviates from the basic power-transition model. Both world wars have been great confrontations between the powers that strove primarily for overseas colonialism and liberal world economy on the one side, and powers that strove for continental military and economic expansion on the other. Wars between Germany and the Soviet Union have been an exception to this rule, but they may be interpreted as struggles for continental dominance. Contrary to various popular theories, seafaring, free-trading, and colonially expanding capitalist powers were able to manage their mutual conflict of interests and turn against the continental power center that was about to acquire a major naval capability (Krippendorff 1975, 127–30).

In world wars, the winning coalition has comprised the leading maritime powers and their allies. The economy of the new hegemonic power has remained intact during the war and is therefore able to subsidize its allies in postwar reconstruction. Goldstein reasons that challenges "are rooted in the previous hegemonic wars," and that new challengers emerge from the winning coalition of that war. The rise of a challenger may take a century to mature; "It is not a sudden lunge for power, an attempted coup" (Goldstein 1985, 345–47).

However, it is pertinent to recall that hegemonic war is not started by this challenger, which joins the coalition with the declining hegemonic power and deliberately organizes its power position during the war. Provided that the present coalitions in world politics persist, this suggests that the next power to challenge the United States would be Japan or China rather than the Soviet Union.

The power-transition theory has obvious relevance for explaining the warfare between major powers, but it must be stressed that hegemonic transition as an economic process and the occurrence of war in major-power relations call for different explanatory theories. Such theories may focus, for example, on capital accumulation and technological innovation on the one hand and on geopolitical ideas on the other. Neither the hegemonic transition itself nor its driving forces can account for the outbreak of major wars. Other approaches are required as well. In other words, there is a need for differentiated theory building in this field.

This call is justified for one simple reason. Periods of hegemonic dominance have not produced a genuine *pax hegemonica*. Both the challengers and the hegemon have been involved in warfare. A further reason for caution is that since 1815 no wars between major powers have been fought during the period of hegemonic decline. There may be a lag between the changes in the distribution of power and its impact on political and military relations between leading states (Väyrynen 1983, 413–14). Power transition is an intriguing and useful way to approach the problem of war between major powers, but it is hardly able to provide a satisfactory explanation of the past, much less the future.

REFERENCES

Beasley, W. G. 1987. *Japanese Imperialism, 1894–1945*. Oxford: Clarendon Press.
Beaud, Michael. 1981. *Histoire du capitalisme, 1500–1980*. Paris: Editions du Seuil.
Beenstock, Michael. 1983. *The World Economy in Transition*. London: Allen and Unwin.
Bousquet, Nicole. 1980. "From Hegemony to Competition: Cycles of the Core." In *Processes of the World System*, edited by Terence K. Hopkins and Immanuel Wallerstein, 46–83. Beverly Hills: Sage Publications.
Capie, Forrest. 1983. *Depression and Protectionism: Britain between the Wars*. London: Allen and Unwin.
Deist, Wilhelm. 1981. *The Wehrmacht and German Rearmament*. Toronto: University of Toronto Press.
Geyer, Michael. 1984. *Deutsche Rüstungspolitík, 1860–1980*. Frankfurt am Main: Suhrkamp.
———. 1985. "The Dynamics of Military Revisionism in the Interwar Years: Military Politics between Rearmament and Diplomacy." In *The German Military in the Age of Total War*, edited by Wilhelm Deist, 100–151. Leamington Spa: Berg.
Gillard, David. 1977. *The Struggle for Asia, 1828–1914: A Study in British and Russian Imperialism*. London: Methuen.
Gilpin, Robert. 1981. *War and Change in World Politics*. Cambridge: Cambridge University Press.
Goldstein, Joshua S. 1985. "Kondratieff Waves as War Cycles." *International Studies Quarterly* 29:411–44.
———. 1988. *Long Cycles: Prosperity and War in the Modern Age*. New Haven: Yale University Press.
Gourevitch, Peter. 1986. *Politics in Hard Times: Comparative Responses to International Economic Crises*. Ithaca, N.Y.: Cornell University Press.
Headrick, Daniel R. 1981. *The Tools of Empire: Technology and European Imperialism in the Nineteenth Century*. Oxford: Oxford University Press.
Hobsbawm, Eric. 1979. *The Age of Capital, 1848–1875*. New York: Mentor Books.
Hopkins, Terence K., and Immanuel Wallerstein. 1979. "Cyclical Rhythms and Secular Trends of the Capitalist World-Economy: Some Premises, Hypotheses, and Questions." *Review* 2:483–500.
Houweling, Henk, and Jan G. Siccama. 1988. "Power Transitions as a Cause of War." *Journal of Conflict Resolution* 32:87–102.

Howard, Michael. 1976. *War in European History*. Oxford: Oxford University Press.

Kennedy, Paul. 1982. *The Rise of the Anglo-German Antagonism, 1860–1914*. London: Allen and Unwin.

———. 1984. "The First World War and the International Power System." *International Security* 9:7–40.

———. 1987. *The Rise and Fall of the Great Powers: Economic Change and Military Conflict from 1500 to 2000*. New York: Random House.

Keohane, Robert O. 1983. "Associative American Development, 1776–1860: Economic Growth and Political Disintegration." In *The Antinomies of Interdependence: National Welfare and the International Division of Labor*, edited by John Gerard Ruggie, 43–90. New York: Columbia University Press.

Kleinknecht, Alfred. 1981. "Lange Welle oder Wechsellagen? Einige methodenkritische Anmerkungen zur Diskussion." In *Konjunktur, Krise, Gesellschaft*, edited by Dietmar Petzina and Ger van Roon, 107–12. Stuttgart: Klett-Cotta.

Krippendorff, Ekkehart. 1975. *Internationales System als Geschichte*. Frankfurt am Main: Campus Verlag.

Kugler, Jacek, and William Domke. 1986. "Comparing the Strength of Nations." *Comparative Political Studies* 19:39–69.

Kugler, Jacek, and A.F.K. Organski. 1986. "Hegemony and War." Paper presented at the International Studies Association meeting, Anaheim, California.

Levy, Jack S. 1985. "Theories of General War." *World Politics* 37:344–74.

McNeill, William H. 1982. *The Pursuit of Power: Technology, Armed Force, and Society since A.D. 1000*. Chicago: University of Chicago Press.

Maddison, Angus. 1982. *Phases of Capitalist Development*. Oxford: Oxford University Press.

Mandelbaum, Michael. 1981. *The Nuclear Revolution: International Politics before and after Hiroshima*. Cambridge: Cambridge University Press.

Mann, Michael. 1987. "The Roots and Contradictions of Modern Militarism." *New Left Review*, no. 162:35–50.

Menzel, Ulrich. 1985. *Lange Wellen und Hegemonie: Eine Literaturbericht*. Bremen: Projekt Hegemoniekrise und Kriegswahrscheinlichkeit.

Neumann, Stephanie. 1984. "International Stratification and the Third World Military Industries." *International Organization* 38: 167–97.

Organski, A.F.K. 1964. *World Politics*. New York: Alfred A. Knopf.

Pearton, Maurice. 1982. *The Knowledgeable State: Diplomacy, War, and Technology since 1830*. London: Burnett Books.

Porter, Bernard. 1983. *Britain, Europe, and the World, 1850–1982: Delusions of Grandeur*. London: Allen and Unwin.

Sen, Gautam. 1984. *The Military Origins of Industrialisation and International Trade Rivalry*. London: Frances Pinter.

Senghaas, Dieter. 1983. "The Cycles of War and Peace." *Bulletin of Peace Proposals* 14:119–24.

Singer, David J., and Thomas Cusack. 1981. "Periodicity, Inexorability, and Steersmanship in International War." In *From National Development to Global Community: Essays in Honor of Karl W. Deutsch*, edited by Richard L. Merritt and Bruce M. Russett, 404–22. Boston: Allen and Unwin.

Speier, Hans. 1969. "The Social Types of War." In *Social Order and the Risks of War*, edited by Hans Speier, 223–29. Cambridge: MIT Press.

Thompson, William R. 1983. "Cycles, Capabilities, and War: An Ecumenical View." In *Contending Approaches to World System Analysis*, edited by William R. Thompson, 141–64. Beverly Hills: Sage Publications.

Thompson, William R., and Karen A. Rasler. 1986. "The Periodicity of Global Wars: An Empirical Assessment and Validation." Paper presented at the International Studies Association meeting, Anaheim, California.

Thompson, William R. and Gary Zuk. 1972. "War, Inflation and Kontradieff's Long Waves." *Journal of Conflict Resolution* 26:621–44.

Trebilcock, Clive. 1981. *The Industrialization of the Continental Powers, 1780–1914*. London: Longman.

van Duijn, J. J. 1983. *The Long Wave in Economic Life*. London: Allen and Unwin.

van Dyke Robinson, Edward. 1900. "War and Economics in History and Theory." *Political Science Quarterly* 15:581–628.

Varga, Eugen. 1935. *The Great Crisis and Its Political Consequences: Economics and Politics, 1928–1934*. London: Modern Books.

Väyrynen, Raimo. 1983. "Economic Cycles, Power Transitions, Political Management, and Wars between Major Powers." *International Studies Quarterly* 27:389–418.

INDEX

CONTRIBUTORS

TERRY BOSWELL is an assistant professor of sociology at Emory University. He is editor of *Revolution in the World-System*, the companion to this volume, and coeditor of *America's Changing Role in the World-System*. His current research includes a time-series analysis of the effects of world hegemony and long economic waves on the pattern of colonialism and the intensity of war from 1650 to 1968.

JOHN BRUEGGEMANN is a graduate student in sociology at Emory University studying the relative influence of class and race on social solidarity and consciousness of interests.

CHRISTOPHER CHASE-DUNN is a professor of sociology at Johns Hopkins University. He is author of *Global Formation* and is currently comparing kin-based, tributary, and capitalist world-systems.

BYRON L. DAVIS is finishing his doctorate in sociology at the University of Utah. His research interests are in macrosociology. He is currently working as a research scientist for the New York State Psychiatric Institute.

EDWARD L. KICK is an associate professor and chair of the sociology department at the University of Utah. His research focuses on quantitative, macrocomparative sociology.

DAVID KIEFER is an associate professor of economics at the University of Utah. Government behavior, peace research, and discrimination are among the topics of his current research.

EDGAR KISER is an assistant professor of sociology at the University of Washington. He is working on a book on the causes of variations in crown autonomy, state policies, and economic development in early modern Western Europe.

GREGORY MCLAUCHLAN is an assistant professor of political science at the University of Denver. His current research focuses on the relationship between war, technology, and state expansion.

KENNETH O'REILLY is a graduate student in the Department of Sociology, Johns Hopkins University.

ROBERT SCHAEFFER is senior editor at *Greenpeace*. He has a Ph.D. in sociology from the State University of New York at Binghamton and is the author of *Warpaths: The Politics of Partition*.

MIKE SWEAT is a graduate student in sociology at Emory University studying the difference in class consciousness between employees in the public and private sectors.

RAIMO VÄYRYNEN is professor of political science at the University of Helsinki.

Studies in the Political Economy of the World-System (Formerly published as Political Economy of the World-System Annuals)
Series Adviser: Immanuel Wallerstein